Plastic Waste Crisis: Innovative Solutions, Global Action, and Pathways to a Sustainable Future

Copyright

Plastic Waste Crisis: Innovative Solutions, Global Action, and Pathways to a Sustainable Future

© 2025 Robert C. Brears

Published by **Global Climate Solutions**

ISBN: 978-1-991369-07-9 (eBook)

ISBN: 978-1-991369-08-6 (Paperback)

Table of Contents

Preface

The world is at a critical juncture in its battle against plastic pollution. Decades of unchecked plastic production and consumption have resulted in a crisis that threatens ecosystems, human health, and economies. With millions of tons of plastic waste accumulating annually in landfills, waterways, and oceans, urgent action is required at all levels—government, industry, and individual behavior.

This book, *Plastic Waste Crisis: Innovative Solutions, Global Action, and Pathways to a Sustainable Future*, is a comprehensive exploration of the issue, providing an in-depth analysis of the environmental, economic, and social consequences of plastic pollution. More importantly, it presents actionable solutions that align with global sustainability goals, technological advancements, and policy frameworks designed to reduce plastic waste and transition toward a circular economy.

The fight against plastic pollution requires collaboration and commitment. While bans on single-use plastics, improved waste management, and innovative materials offer promising pathways, systemic change must be driven by regulatory enforcement, corporate accountability, and public engagement. As this book demonstrates, a multi-stakeholder approach is essential to reversing the damage already inflicted and ensuring a more sustainable future for generations to come.

It is time to move beyond incremental change and embrace a transformative shift in how plastics are produced, consumed, and disposed of. The solutions exist—what remains is the will to implement them at scale.

Robert C. Brears

Introduction

Plastic waste has become one of the most pressing environmental issues of our time. As a material designed for convenience and durability, plastics have infiltrated every aspect of modern life, from packaging and consumer goods to industrial applications. However, the very properties that make plastics so useful have also led to their accumulation in the environment, causing widespread pollution in oceans, landscapes, and ecosystems. This book seeks to explore the global crisis of plastic waste, providing a comprehensive understanding of its causes, impacts, and potential solutions.

The introduction begins by outlining the scope of the plastic waste problem, examining how plastic production has surged over the past century, leading to a dramatic increase in waste. It delves into the far-reaching effects of plastic pollution, from its harmful impact on marine life and ecosystems to the human health risks posed by exposure to plastic chemicals. Additionally, the economic burden of plastic waste is significant, with costs related to cleanup, waste management, and losses in tourism and fishing industries.

This book also introduces the various solutions that have been proposed and implemented to mitigate the plastic waste crisis. From global policy frameworks to innovative technologies, it explores efforts to reduce plastic production, increase recycling, and shift toward sustainable alternatives. Ultimately, this introduction sets the stage for a deeper examination of the plastic waste crisis, offering readers insights into the urgent need for coordinated action across governments, industries, and individuals to address the challenge and pave the way toward a cleaner, more sustainable future.

Overview of Plastic Waste as a Global Environmental Crisis

Plastic waste is one of the most pervasive environmental challenges of the modern era. With its widespread use in packaging, consumer products, and industrial applications, plastic has become a ubiquitous material in everyday life. However, the convenience, durability, and low cost of plastic are precisely the factors that contribute to its environmental impact. Plastic, while immensely useful, is slow to decompose, and much of it ends up in landfills, oceans, rivers, and ecosystems, where it can persist for centuries.

The roots of the plastic waste crisis lie in the exponential growth of plastic production over the past few decades. According to the United Nations, more than 300 million tons of plastic are produced each year, with a significant portion being used for short-lived, single-use items. These include plastic bags, bottles, food wrappers, and straws, which are often discarded after a single use, contributing to an overwhelming accumulation of waste. Unlike organic materials, plastics do not biodegrade naturally and instead break down into smaller particles, known as microplastics, which continue to pollute the environment and enter the food chain.

Plastic waste is not confined to a specific region or country; it is a global problem. Developed nations, with their high consumption rates, are some of the largest producers of plastic waste, but many developing countries, especially those without effective waste management systems, face severe challenges in dealing with the influx of plastic waste. Inadequate waste collection and recycling systems, particularly in countries with rapidly growing urban populations, exacerbate the problem. Plastic waste often ends up in rivers and oceans, where it contributes to the formation of massive garbage patches, such as the Great Pacific Garbage Patch, which is estimated to be twice the size of Texas.

The environmental consequences of plastic waste are severe. Marine animals, from fish and seabirds to turtles and whales, are at risk of ingesting plastic debris, which can lead to injury, poisoning, or death. In fact, research has shown that nearly 700 marine species are threatened by plastic pollution, with many species consuming plastic either intentionally or accidentally. Moreover, plastics can leach toxic chemicals into the water, which can harm aquatic ecosystems and enter the food chain, impacting both wildlife and human populations.

In addition to its impact on marine and terrestrial ecosystems, plastic waste poses significant human health risks. Chemicals used in the production of plastics, such as bisphenol A (BPA) and phthalates, have been linked to a range of health problems, including hormone disruption, developmental issues, and certain cancers. The pervasive nature of plastic waste means that these chemicals are now present in air, water, and soil, making it increasingly difficult to avoid exposure.

The economic costs associated with plastic waste are substantial. Governments and businesses spend billions of dollars each year on waste management, cleanup efforts, and addressing the environmental damages caused by plastic pollution. Industries such as tourism, fishing, and agriculture are also affected by the plastic crisis. For instance, the tourism industry faces losses from the aesthetic and ecological degradation of popular coastal destinations, while the fishing industry suffers from the impact of plastic pollution on marine life and fishing gear.

As the problem of plastic waste continues to grow, the urgency to find sustainable solutions has never been greater. Addressing plastic waste requires a multi-pronged approach that involves governments, businesses, and individuals working together to reduce plastic production, improve waste management, and promote alternative materials. It is clear that without concerted action, the consequences of plastic pollution will continue to escalate, with profound implications for the environment, human health, and economies worldwide.

Importance of Addressing Plastic Waste and Its Effects on Ecosystems, Human Health, and Economies

Addressing plastic waste is of critical importance because of its widespread and lasting effects on ecosystems, human health, and economies. The pervasive nature of plastic pollution means that the consequences are far-reaching and multifaceted, affecting every aspect of life on Earth. With millions of tons of plastic being produced and discarded each year, it is essential to recognize and confront the dire impacts this waste has on both the environment and society.

First and foremost, plastic waste poses a severe threat to ecosystems worldwide. Plastics, particularly single-use items like bags, bottles, and straws, take centuries to decompose, and during this period, they can disrupt natural habitats. In terrestrial ecosystems, animals can become entangled in plastic waste, leading to injury and death. On land, plastic debris also contributes to soil degradation and can harm plant life by blocking light and restricting water absorption. But the most visible and devastating impact is found in our oceans. It is estimated that 8 million metric tons of plastic enter the ocean annually, causing significant harm to marine life. Marine animals, from sea turtles to whales, ingest or become entangled in plastics, leading to suffocation, starvation, and poisoning. Plastics break down into microplastics, which are consumed by a wide range of marine species and can travel up the food chain, threatening biodiversity and destabilizing aquatic ecosystems.

Beyond the environmental impacts, plastic waste has direct consequences on human health. The chemicals used in plastic production, such as BPA and phthalates, are known to disrupt hormonal systems and are linked to numerous health problems, including reproductive issues, developmental defects, and even certain cancers. These harmful substances leach into food, water, and air as plastics degrade in the environment. Microplastics have now been detected in drinking water, food products, and even in the air, making human exposure nearly inevitable. Recent studies have shown that microplastics are present in human tissues, raising concerns about their potential long-term health effects, particularly as plastics continue to accumulate in the environment. The ingestion of plastic waste by marine species also poses risks to human health, as people who consume contaminated seafood may inadvertently consume microplastics and associated toxins.

The economic consequences of plastic waste are also profound. Governments around the world are spending vast sums of money on waste management and cleanup efforts, but the costs far exceed the resources allocated to tackling the problem. Plastic waste strains waste management systems, particularly in developing countries where proper recycling infrastructure is often lacking. The financial burden of cleaning up plastic waste and removing it from oceans and landscapes is staggering, with estimates reaching billions of dollars annually. The tourism industry also suffers due to the aesthetic and environmental degradation of coastal and rural areas, leading to reduced tourism revenues. Similarly, the fishing industry is affected by the ingestion of plastics by marine life and the damage caused to fishing gear by plastic debris. The growing burden on businesses to find sustainable packaging solutions and manage waste effectively also adds to the economic toll.

Addressing the plastic waste crisis is not only a matter of environmental preservation but also human well-being and economic stability. The current trajectory of plastic production and waste accumulation is unsustainable, and without meaningful action, the consequences will worsen. Governments, industries, and individuals must work together to reduce plastic consumption, improve waste management, and adopt sustainable alternatives. In doing so, we can mitigate the devastating effects of plastic waste and ensure a healthier, more sustainable future for generations to come.

Structure of the Book and Introduction to the Solutions Presented

This book is structured to provide a comprehensive understanding of the plastic waste crisis, examining its causes, impacts, and, most importantly, the pathways toward solutions. It is divided into seven chapters, each addressing a different aspect of the issue while building a broader narrative around how we can collectively tackle the plastic waste crisis. From understanding the global scale of the problem to exploring innovative solutions, the structure is designed to offer both knowledge and actionable insights.

The first chapter, "The Plastic Waste Crisis," lays the foundation for the discussion by providing a detailed overview of plastic production and consumption patterns, tracing the history of plastic use, and explaining the life cycle of plastic waste. It covers the environmental, health, and economic impacts of plastic waste, emphasizing the severity of the crisis. This chapter serves to highlight the urgency of the issue and set the stage for understanding why solutions are essential.

In Chapter 2: Global Policy and Regulatory Responses, the focus shifts to the various efforts made by governments, international bodies, and organizations to combat plastic waste. It provides an overview of international agreements, such as the United Nations Sustainable Development Goals (SDGs), and explores national and regional policies that are beginning to address plastic waste, such as bans on single-use plastics and Extended Producer Responsibility (EPR) laws. This chapter also looks at the challenges faced in implementing these policies, such as political resistance and enforcement issues, offering a critical view of the effectiveness of existing regulatory frameworks.

Chapter 3: The Role of Industry in Plastic Waste dives into the contribution of industries, particularly the plastic production, packaging, and consumer goods sectors, to the plastic waste problem. This chapter examines the push towards fossil fuel-based plastic production, the prevalence of single-use plastics in packaging, and corporate responsibility initiatives. It also addresses the issue of "greenwashing," where companies falsely present themselves as environmentally responsible, without substantial changes to their practices. This chapter serves as a call to action for industries to move beyond superficial efforts and adopt genuine, sustainable practices.

The fourth chapter, "Plastic Waste Management and Recycling," tackles the complexities of dealing with plastic waste once it has been generated. It discusses the global state of plastic recycling, technological innovations in recycling, and the challenges faced in improving recycling rates. The chapter also explores waste-to-energy technologies and their potential as part of the solution, along with the principles of zero-waste and circular economy models, which aim to reduce waste and encourage recycling by design.

Chapter 5: Pathways to Reducing Plastic Waste presents a forward-looking perspective, offering practical solutions to the plastic waste crisis. It examines the power of individual behavioral change, the importance of consumer awareness, and the role of education in shifting public attitudes. The chapter also covers innovations in alternative materials, such as plant-based plastics and biodegradable alternatives, and explores corporate responsibility and collaboration between governments, businesses, and civil society. Key technological breakthroughs and policy measures are also discussed, providing a roadmap for long-term solutions.

Chapter 6: Case Studies in Plastic Waste Management offers a look at successful global and community-level models for reducing plastic waste. By presenting examples from different countries, cities, and organizations, this chapter illustrates the practical application of solutions. It highlights grassroots movements and innovative industry solutions, showcasing how cooperation at all levels can lead to meaningful change.

The final chapter, "The Future of Plastic Waste," explores the potential future trends in plastic waste production and pollution. It presents innovative solutions on the horizon, including new technologies, materials, and policy developments. The chapter concludes with a call for urgent global action, emphasizing the need for international cooperation to mitigate the growing plastic crisis.

Throughout the book, the solutions presented are varied, practical, and actionable, with a focus on reducing plastic waste at every stage of its lifecycle—from production to disposal. By exploring global policy, industry roles, technological innovations, and grassroots efforts, this book provides a comprehensive roadmap for tackling one of the most pressing environmental issues of our time.

Chapter 1: The Plastic Waste Crisis

Chapter 1 provides an in-depth exploration of the global plastic waste crisis, setting the stage for understanding the full scope and severity of the issue. This chapter begins by tracing the rise of plastic production and consumption over the past century, highlighting how plastic became an integral part of modern life. It examines the life cycle of plastic, from its production to its widespread use in consumer goods, and the inevitable disposal problems that follow.

The chapter also delves into the environmental impacts of plastic waste, focusing on the detrimental effects on both terrestrial and marine ecosystems. It discusses the accumulation of plastic debris in oceans, such as the Great Pacific Garbage Patch, and the dangers posed by microplastics to marine life and food chains. Additionally, the chapter explores the human health risks associated with plastic exposure, from toxic chemicals in plastic products to the risks of microplastic contamination in the food supply.

Finally, the economic costs of plastic waste are examined, including the financial burden on governments, businesses, and industries that are grappling with the growing amounts of plastic waste. By presenting a clear picture of the crisis, this chapter underscores the urgent need for comprehensive solutions to address the plastic waste problem.

Global Plastic Production and Consumption

The rise of plastic use over the past century has been one of the most significant developments in material science, fundamentally altering industries, economies, and daily life. Plastics, first introduced in the early 20th century, revolutionized the way products were made and consumed. Initially, the production of plastics was relatively small-scale, with the first synthetic plastic, Bakelite, created in 1907, followed by other early plastics like polystyrene and polyethylene in the 1920s and 1930s. These early plastics paved the way for the material's widespread adoption due to their low cost, versatility, and the ability to be molded into various shapes and forms.

The real expansion of plastic production began in the post-World War II era. Advancements in polymer chemistry, along with the development of new plastic materials, led to a boom in plastic use, particularly in packaging, consumer goods, and the automotive sector. By the 1950s and 1960s, the mass production of plastics had taken off, and plastics began replacing more traditional materials such as glass, metal, and wood in various industries. The introduction of plastics like polyethylene, polypropylene, and PVC (polyvinyl chloride) offered a combination of durability, flexibility, and lightweight properties, making them ideal for a wide range of applications.

By the 1980s and 1990s, plastics had become integral to virtually every sector. The material was not only used in packaging and consumer goods but also in electronics, medical equipment, textiles, and even construction. The convenience and affordability of plastic products led to an explosion in demand, and global plastic production skyrocketed. According to the United Nations, annual plastic production has reached more than 300 million tons, with over 40% of this production used for packaging alone. Packaging, especially for food and beverage products, is one of the largest contributors to plastic waste, as plastic packaging is designed to be used briefly before being discarded.

The key industries driving global plastic consumption are numerous and span a wide range of sectors. Packaging remains the largest consumer of plastic, accounting for nearly 40% of global plastic production. In particular, the food and beverage industry has created a massive demand for single-use plastic items, such as bottles, bags, and wrappers. Plastics are favored in packaging because they are inexpensive, lightweight, and can be molded into any shape, allowing for easy transport and storage. However, the disposable nature of plastic packaging has contributed to a growing waste problem, as much of this plastic is used once and then discarded, often without being recycled.

The automotive industry is another major consumer of plastics. The use of plastics in vehicles has increased significantly over the years, replacing metals and glass in various parts of cars, trucks, and buses. Plastics are used in components such as dashboards, bumpers, interior panels, and engine parts due to their lightweight nature, which helps reduce fuel consumption and improve vehicle efficiency. In fact, modern vehicles contain hundreds of pounds of plastic materials, contributing to the overall increase in global plastic consumption.

Textiles also drive plastic consumption through synthetic fibers such as polyester, nylon, and acrylic. These fibers, made from petroleum-based plastic, are used in a wide range of clothing, upholstery, and carpets. The global fast fashion industry has significantly increased demand for these materials, as synthetic fibers are cheap to produce and offer durability and ease of care. However, the environmental impact of synthetic textiles is considerable, as they shed microplastics when washed, which enter the environment and oceans.

Medical and healthcare products are another critical sector driving plastic consumption. Plastics are used extensively in medical devices, syringes, IV bags, surgical instruments, and diagnostic equipment. The healthcare industry relies on plastic for its sterile properties, light weight, and cost-effectiveness. Single-use plastic medical products are common, which presents a challenge in terms of waste management.

The electronics industry also contributes to plastic consumption, with plastics used in everything from smartphones and computers to televisions and household appliances. The demand for lightweight and durable plastics in electronic devices has grown alongside the increase in consumer technology use globally.

The Life Cycle of Plastic Waste

The life cycle of plastic waste is a critical concept in understanding the environmental impact of plastic production, consumption, and disposal. Plastics, derived primarily from fossil fuels, undergo a complex process from production to eventual disposal. The life cycle of plastic begins with the extraction of raw materials, followed by its transformation into various plastic products, usage by consumers, and disposal at the end of its useful life. Unfortunately, this life cycle often ends in waste accumulation, which poses significant challenges to ecosystems, human health, and economies.

Production of plastic begins with the extraction of petroleum and natural gas, which are the primary raw materials for plastic production. These fossil fuels are refined into monomers, which are the building blocks for plastics. Various polymerization processes then combine these monomers into long chains, creating different types of plastic, such as polyethylene, polypropylene, and PVC. These materials are highly versatile and can be molded, extruded, or formed into a wide variety of products. The global plastic production process has grown exponentially over the past few decades, with annual production now exceeding 300 million tons. This rapid increase in production is driven by the high demand for plastic across many industries, including packaging, construction, automotive, electronics, and textiles.

Once produced, plastics are distributed for usage in consumer goods, packaging, and industrial applications. Plastics' durability, flexibility, and low cost make them the material of choice for a wide range of products. In fact, plastic is used in nearly every sector of the global economy, including food and beverage packaging, medical supplies, clothing, and household items. The material's versatility and convenience have led to its widespread adoption, with single-use plastics becoming particularly prevalent in packaging. Plastics are often used in packaging because they protect products from contamination, are lightweight, and can be mass-produced at low cost. Common plastic items such as bottles, bags, straws, and food containers are used for just a short period before being discarded.

However, the disposal of plastic waste is where significant environmental challenges arise. Unlike organic materials, plastics do not biodegrade, meaning they can persist in the environment for hundreds of years. Instead of breaking down naturally, plastics break into smaller pieces called microplastics, which continue to pollute the environment. While recycling offers a potential solution to managing plastic waste, the reality is that only a small percentage of plastic is actually recycled. According to estimates, less than 10% of plastic waste is recycled globally. Much of the remaining plastic waste ends up in landfills, where it can take centuries to decompose. Even more concerning, large quantities of plastic waste find their way into oceans, rivers, and landscapes, where it harms wildlife and ecosystems.

One of the most problematic aspects of the plastic life cycle is the widespread use of single-use plastics. Single-use plastics are designed to be used once and then discarded, often after only a brief period of use. Common examples of single-use plastics include plastic bags, straws, utensils, and food packaging. These items are typically made from low-cost plastics that are convenient and lightweight, making them ideal for disposable applications. The problem with single-use plastics is that they are not intended for reuse or recycling, yet they often end up in waste streams, where they are either not recycled or not properly managed.

The environmental impact of single-use plastics is particularly severe. These plastics are not only responsible for large amounts of plastic waste but also for significant pollution in oceans and waterways. Sea creatures, including fish, sea turtles, and marine mammals, often ingest or become entangled in plastic waste, leading to injury or death. Microplastics, which result from the breakdown of larger plastic items, are ingested by marine organisms, entering the food chain and ultimately reaching humans. As a result, single-use plastics represent one of the most pressing environmental concerns associated with plastic waste.

Environmental Impacts of Plastic Waste

The environmental impacts of plastic waste are profound and far-reaching, affecting both terrestrial and marine ecosystems. Plastics are non-biodegradable, which means that once they are discarded, they can persist in the environment for centuries, causing significant harm to wildlife and ecosystems. As plastic waste continues to accumulate globally, its negative effects on biodiversity, habitats, and natural resources have become an increasingly urgent environmental issue.

Effects on Terrestrial and Marine Ecosystems

Plastic waste has a major impact on both terrestrial and marine ecosystems. On land, plastic pollution is a visible and growing problem in urban areas, forests, and rural landscapes. Wildlife often becomes entangled in plastic debris, such as plastic bags, six-pack rings, and fishing nets. This entanglement can lead to suffocation, injury, or death. In addition to physical harm, animals may also ingest plastic, mistaking it for food. This ingestion of plastic can lead to internal blockages, malnutrition, or poisoning due to toxic chemicals that leach from the plastic. Terrestrial animals, such as birds, mammals, and small rodents, are particularly vulnerable to the detrimental effects of plastic pollution, as they often encounter discarded plastic in their natural habitats.

Marine ecosystems are especially vulnerable to plastic pollution. The oceans are the final destination for a significant portion of the world's plastic waste, with millions of tons of plastic entering the seas each year. Marine species, including fish, seabirds, turtles, and whales, are at risk of ingesting plastic debris, which can lead to serious health consequences. When plastics are ingested, they can block digestive tracts, causing starvation or malnutrition. In some cases, plastics can also release harmful chemicals into the environment, further threatening marine life. The physical presence of plastic in the oceans also disrupts natural habitats, such as coral reefs and seabeds, by smothering marine life and obstructing important ecological processes.

Plastic Pollution in Oceans: The Great Pacific Garbage Patch

One of the most well-known examples of plastic pollution in the ocean is the Great Pacific Garbage Patch, a vast area of debris located between Hawaii and California. This patch is not a solid mass of waste but rather a collection of small plastic particles and larger debris trapped by ocean currents in what is known as the North Pacific Gyre. The Great Pacific Garbage Patch is estimated to be twice the size of Texas and is just one example of the larger problem of plastic pollution in the world's oceans. Other major oceanic garbage patches exist in different parts of the world, including the Atlantic and Indian Oceans, all of which contain staggering amounts of plastic waste.

The Great Pacific Garbage Patch is a critical issue because it is not just a concentration of floating debris; it also serves as a symbol of the growing accumulation of plastic in the oceans. This pollution affects a wide range of marine species that either become entangled in the debris or ingest the plastic. The toxic chemicals that plastics release into the ocean further exacerbate the damage to marine ecosystems. The long-term consequences of these pollution hotspots are devastating, as they impact biodiversity, fisheries, and the health of the oceans, which are crucial for supporting life on Earth.

Microplastics and Their Long-Term Impact

As plastic waste breaks down in the environment, it doesn't simply disappear. Instead, it degrades into smaller particles known as microplastics—plastic fragments less than 5 millimeters in size. These microplastics are a significant environmental threat because they are so small that they are nearly impossible to remove from the environment once they have been released. Microplastics are ubiquitous, found in oceans, rivers, lakes, and even in the air. They are easily consumed by marine organisms, ranging from plankton to larger fish and mammals. When microplastics are ingested, they can accumulate in the bodies of animals, leading to toxic effects and potentially harming entire food chains.

Microplastics have also been found in tap water, bottled water, and various food products, raising concerns about their impact on human health. Although research on the health effects of microplastics in humans is still in its early stages, there is growing evidence that these particles could pose risks, including the potential for chemical toxicity and the disruption of biological processes. The accumulation of microplastics in the environment has led to calls for better waste management, recycling, and alternatives to plastic products.

The long-term environmental impact of plastic waste, particularly microplastics, is still not fully understood, but the persistence of plastic pollution in ecosystems suggests that the damage could be irreversible unless immediate action is taken. To address this growing environmental crisis, efforts must be made to reduce plastic consumption, improve waste management, and increase recycling rates. Additionally, there is a pressing need for the development of alternative, biodegradable materials that can reduce the long-lasting impact of plastic waste on terrestrial and marine ecosystems.

Human Health Impacts

Plastic pollution not only threatens the environment but also poses significant risks to human health. Plastics contain a variety of chemicals that can leach into the environment and, through ingestion or exposure, enter the human body. These chemicals, including BPA and phthalates, are known to have harmful effects on human health. As plastic waste continues to accumulate in landfills, oceans, and other environments, the potential for human exposure to these toxic substances grows, creating serious concerns for public health.

Exposure to Chemicals from Plastics (BPA, Phthalates)

One of the primary concerns regarding plastic and human health is the presence of toxic chemicals, such as BPA and phthalates, which are often used in the production of plastics. BPA is a chemical used to make polycarbonate plastics and epoxy resins, commonly found in products such as plastic bottles, food containers, and water bottles.

BPA is known to be an endocrine disruptor, meaning it can interfere with the body's hormone systems. Research has linked BPA exposure to a range of health problems, including reproductive issues, developmental delays in children, and an increased risk of certain cancers. BPA can leach into food and beverages from plastic containers, particularly when they are heated or subjected to wear and tear, thus making its presence in the environment a significant public health concern.

Similarly, phthalates, a group of chemicals used to soften and increase the flexibility of plastics, are commonly found in products such as vinyl flooring, shower curtains, and children's toys. Phthalates have been linked to a variety of health issues, including hormone imbalances, respiratory problems, and developmental defects in children. These chemicals are also considered endocrine disruptors and can interfere with normal hormone functions. Phthalates can leach out of plastic products over time, especially when they are exposed to heat or wear, and have been detected in the air, water, and food products. As these chemicals are widespread in the environment, human exposure occurs through ingestion, inhalation, and skin contact.

Another concerning issue is the presence of microplastics—small plastic particles that result from the breakdown of larger plastic items. Microplastics have been found in food, drinking water, and even in the air, leading to the question of how much humans are exposed to these tiny particles. Though research is still ongoing, early studies suggest that microplastics may carry harmful chemicals on their surfaces, potentially increasing their toxicity. This exposure can occur through the consumption of contaminated seafood, drinking water, or even through the inhalation of microplastic particles in the air, especially in urban environments.

The Connection Between Plastic Pollution and Human Health Risks

Plastic pollution is intrinsically linked to human health risks in multiple ways. The chemicals in plastics, such as BPA and phthalates, can leach into food, water, and the environment, causing chronic exposure over time. The impact of plastic pollution on human health is particularly concerning in the context of increasing plastic production and waste. As plastic products degrade in landfills and oceans, they break down into smaller pieces, including microplastics, which can enter the food chain when ingested by marine organisms.

Humans are exposed to plastic pollutants through the consumption of seafood, drinking water, and the inhalation of microplastics from the air. Studies have shown that marine life, including fish and shellfish, often ingest microplastics, mistaking them for food. When humans consume contaminated seafood, they too ingest microplastics, which can accumulate in their bodies over time. Research has shown that microplastics can travel through the human gastrointestinal tract and may even enter the bloodstream, potentially leading to harmful health effects. Ingesting plastic waste has been linked to inflammation, cell damage, and increased oxidative stress, which could contribute to the development of various diseases, including cancers and cardiovascular diseases.

In addition to ingestion, exposure to plastic pollution through inhalation is an emerging concern. Microplastics have been found in the air, particularly in urban areas, where they are released from plastic waste, tire dust, and synthetic fibers in clothing. When inhaled, these particles may contribute to respiratory issues such as asthma, bronchitis, and even chronic obstructive pulmonary disease (COPD). The effects of long-term exposure to airborne microplastics are still not fully understood, but there is growing evidence that they may have detrimental effects on lung tissue and overall respiratory health.

Furthermore, the environmental persistence of plastics means that plastic pollution will continue to affect human health for generations to come. As plastics accumulate in the environment and continue to degrade into smaller particles, the risk of human exposure increases.

The widespread presence of plastic pollutants in our food and water supply highlights the need for urgent action to reduce plastic production and waste, as well as to find alternative materials that are safer for both the environment and human health.

Economic Costs of Plastic Waste

The economic costs of plastic waste are vast and multifaceted, imposing a significant financial burden on governments, businesses, and industries worldwide. As plastic waste continues to accumulate in landfills, oceans, and other environments, its economic impact has become increasingly apparent. The costs related to managing plastic waste, conducting clean-up efforts, and addressing damage to critical sectors such as tourism, fishing, and marine industries are substantial. These financial strains highlight the urgent need for a global effort to reduce plastic production, improve waste management, and shift toward sustainable alternatives.

The Financial Burden on Governments and Businesses

Governments around the world bear a significant financial burden as they are responsible for waste management and the cleanup of plastic pollution. In many countries, public funds are allocated to waste management programs that aim to collect, recycle, or dispose of plastic waste. However, despite the efforts made, the growing volume of plastic waste often exceeds the capacity of existing waste management infrastructure. The costs associated with maintaining and expanding waste management systems, including landfill sites, recycling facilities, and waste-to-energy plants, continue to rise. According to the World Economic Forum, the cost of waste management, including the disposal and recycling of plastics, is estimated at hundreds of billions of dollars annually, and this figure is expected to increase as plastic consumption grows.

The financial burden on businesses is also significant, particularly for companies that rely on plastic packaging. Many companies face pressure from consumers, environmental organizations, and governments to reduce their use of single-use plastics and adopt more sustainable practices. The transition to sustainable packaging solutions, such as biodegradable or recyclable alternatives, often comes with higher production costs. Additionally, businesses are increasingly investing in waste management systems to ensure that their plastic waste is properly disposed of or recycled. For many companies, the cost of managing plastic waste is passed down the supply chain, with businesses that produce and distribute plastic products bearing a substantial share of the financial responsibility.

Costs Related to Clean-up Efforts and Waste Management

One of the most direct and visible economic costs associated with plastic waste is the cost of clean-up efforts. Governments, local authorities, and environmental organizations worldwide are spending vast amounts of money to clean up plastic waste from landfills, streets, and natural environments, especially in areas where waste management systems are inadequate. Efforts to remove plastic debris from rivers, beaches, and urban areas can be labor-intensive and costly. For example, it is estimated that the cost of cleaning up plastic waste in the United States alone exceeds $11 billion annually. Much of this money is spent on waste collection, transportation, and disposal, which could be better spent on more sustainable solutions.

In marine environments, the costs of clean-up are particularly high. Plastic waste in oceans is a persistent problem, with large-scale clean-up projects required to remove debris from the water. The Great Pacific Garbage Patch, which contains millions of tons of plastic, is just one example of the massive cleanup efforts needed to address ocean plastic pollution. Specialized vessels and teams are often deployed to retrieve plastic waste from the sea, a costly process that requires coordination among governments, non-governmental organizations, and businesses. While these efforts are necessary to protect marine life and ecosystems, they represent a significant drain on resources that could be better used for preventive measures and long-term solutions.

Damage to Tourism, Fishing, and Marine Industries

The economic impact of plastic waste extends beyond waste management and clean-up efforts. Industries that rely on clean environments, such as tourism and fishing, are particularly vulnerable to the negative effects of plastic pollution. The tourism industry, for example, is heavily affected by the presence of plastic waste on beaches, in waterways, and in natural landscapes. Polluted beaches and contaminated coastal areas discourage tourists from visiting, leading to a decline in tourism revenues. In some regions, particularly those dependent on eco-tourism, the presence of plastic waste can harm a destination's reputation and result in long-term economic losses. For instance, studies have shown that plastic pollution on beaches can lead to a decline in tourism numbers, which directly impacts local businesses, employment, and national economies.

The fishing industry is another sector heavily impacted by plastic waste. Marine life often ingests plastic debris or becomes entangled in it, which can lead to population declines and affect fish stocks. Additionally, plastic waste can damage fishing gear, such as nets and lines, leading to costly repairs and replacements. In some regions, the presence of plastic waste in the oceans has led to restrictions on fishing areas or reduced fish catch sizes, further damaging the economic viability of the industry. Moreover, the contamination of seafood with microplastics poses a threat to human health, further impacting the market for fish and seafood products.

The damage to marine ecosystems caused by plastic pollution also affects industries that rely on healthy oceans and coastal areas, such as aquaculture, shipping, and marine research. The loss of biodiversity, disruption of ecosystems, and degradation of marine habitats can result in significant financial losses for industries and economies dependent on the health of marine resources.

Chapter 2: Global Policy and Regulatory Responses

Chapter 2 examines the global policy landscape surrounding plastic waste and the various regulatory frameworks that have been developed to combat this growing crisis. This chapter provides an in-depth analysis of international agreements, national policies, and regional initiatives that aim to reduce plastic pollution and promote more sustainable practices. It highlights key efforts by global organizations such as the United Nations, as well as the role of international bodies like UNEP, the G7, and the G20 in addressing plastic waste through collective action.

Additionally, the chapter delves into the evolving national and regional responses, including plastic bans, EPR laws, and other regulations designed to reduce plastic use and increase recycling. Despite these efforts, the implementation of policies often faces significant challenges, including inconsistent enforcement, political resistance, and the complexity of managing the global plastic supply chain. This chapter explores these obstacles while emphasizing the importance of cohesive, well-enforced policies that can drive meaningful change in the fight against plastic pollution.

International Agreements and Efforts

The issue of plastic waste has garnered significant international attention due to its widespread environmental, economic, and health impacts. As a result, global initiatives and international organizations have played crucial roles in addressing plastic pollution. This section explores the key global efforts, including the United Nations' SDGs, as well as the role of international bodies like the United Nations Environment Programme (UNEP) and major political forums like the G7 and G20 in tackling plastic waste and advancing sustainability goals.

Overview of Global Initiatives like the United Nations' SDGs

The United Nations (UN) has long recognized the urgency of addressing environmental pollution, and plastic waste is a key element of this global agenda. In 2015, the UN adopted the SDGs, a set of 17 global objectives aimed at achieving a more sustainable, equitable, and prosperous world by 2030. Among these goals, SDG 14 (Life Below Water) and SDG 12 (Responsible Consumption and Production) directly address plastic pollution, highlighting the need for sustainable management of resources and the protection of oceans from pollution.

SDG 12: Responsible Consumption and Production calls for a shift towards more sustainable production and consumption patterns. Specifically, Target 12.5 aims to substantially reduce waste generation through prevention, reduction, recycling, and reuse by 2030. This target encourages countries to adopt policies that address plastic waste, reduce single-use plastics, and promote circular economy models. The widespread adoption of such measures is essential in reducing the volume of plastic waste and fostering a more sustainable approach to production and consumption.

SDG 14: Life Below Water is focused on the conservation and sustainable use of oceans, seas, and marine resources. Target 14.1, in particular, seeks to prevent and significantly reduce marine pollution of all kinds, including plastic waste, by 2025. This target highlights the importance of reducing plastic pollution in the oceans, which is one of the most visible and concerning impacts of plastic waste. International cooperation is central to achieving this target, as ocean pollution is a global issue that requires coordinated efforts across borders.

The SDGs have provided a comprehensive framework for addressing plastic waste, encouraging governments, businesses, and organizations to commit to tangible actions. Through these goals, the international community has placed greater emphasis on reducing plastic production, improving waste management, and promoting alternatives to harmful plastic products. By aligning global efforts with the SDGs, countries can work towards achieving long-term sustainability and environmental protection.

The Role of International Bodies like UNEP and the G7/G20 in Addressing Plastic Waste

UNEP

The UNEP plays a pivotal role in coordinating global efforts to address plastic pollution. UNEP has been at the forefront of advocating for policies that reduce plastic waste and promote sustainable waste management practices. In 2018, UNEP launched the #CleanSeas campaign, which aims to eliminate major sources of marine litter, including plastics. The campaign encourages governments, businesses, and individuals to take action against plastic pollution by supporting international agreements, improving waste management, and reducing plastic consumption.

UNEP has also been instrumental in guiding countries towards a global agreement on plastic pollution. In 2019, UNEP organized a global conference in Nairobi, where over 180 countries agreed to take steps toward a binding international treaty on plastic waste. The meeting led to the adoption of the Nairobi Declaration, which set the stage for future negotiations on a comprehensive global plastics treaty. UNEP has since been working to shape international negotiations that could lead to stronger, legally binding commitments on plastic pollution reduction and the development of a circular economy.

In addition to these initiatives, UNEP has been a strong advocate for the creation of a Global Plastics Outlook, which tracks the progress of countries in reducing plastic waste and improving recycling. Through data collection, research, and policy recommendations, UNEP helps governments understand the scope of the plastic waste problem and identify actionable solutions.

The G7 and G20

The G7 and G20, two of the world's most influential economic and political forums, have also played significant roles in addressing plastic waste, particularly by fostering international cooperation and setting priorities for global action. Both forums bring together governments of the world's major economies to discuss and agree on critical issues, including environmental sustainability and plastic pollution.

The G7, consisting of seven major industrialized nations, has focused on plastic waste in recent years. At the 2018 G7 Summit in Canada, leaders of the member countries committed to reducing marine plastic litter and promoting a circular economy for plastics. In their Ocean Plastics Charter, the G7 countries pledged to take action to reduce plastic pollution, including measures to reduce single-use plastics, improve waste management, and increase recycling efforts. This commitment has led to initiatives aimed at enhancing the effectiveness of international agreements on plastic pollution, such as supporting UNEP's efforts and backing the development of a global plastics treaty.

Similarly, the G20, which includes a broader group of nations, including both developed and developing countries, has addressed plastic waste through its environmental agenda. The G20 has encouraged its members to develop national strategies for plastic waste management and has promoted international cooperation to reduce plastic pollution. At the 2019 G20 summit in Japan, leaders recognized the need for urgent action on plastic waste and endorsed measures to curb plastic leakage into the ocean. The G20 has continued to prioritize sustainable practices and circular economy models to address plastic pollution while ensuring that developing nations have the resources and support needed to manage plastic waste effectively.

The G7 and G20 play important roles in shaping the global conversation on plastic pollution by providing platforms for international dialogue, setting commitments, and fostering cooperation among governments. These forums continue to push for stronger action on plastic waste and advocate for international frameworks to tackle the problem on a global scale.

National and Regional Policies

In addition to global efforts, national and regional policies are crucial to addressing the growing plastic waste crisis. Governments around the world are implementing various strategies to reduce plastic pollution, with a particular focus on banning single-use plastics and introducing EPR laws. These policies aim to curb the production and consumption of plastic products, enhance recycling efforts, and shift the burden of waste management onto producers. This section will explore the impact of single-use plastic bans in various countries and the implementation of EPR laws as part of the regulatory response to plastic pollution.

Bans on Single-Use Plastics in Various Countries

One of the most direct approaches to tackling plastic pollution is the imposition of bans on single-use plastics. Single-use plastics are disposable products designed to be used once and then discarded, such as plastic bags, straws, cutlery, and packaging. These items make up a significant portion of global plastic waste, especially as they are often not recycled and end up in landfills, incinerators, or the environment.

A number of countries have taken decisive steps to reduce plastic pollution by implementing bans on single-use plastics. For example, Kenya introduced one of the most stringent plastic bag bans in the world in 2017. The ban prohibits the production, sale, and use of plastic bags, with severe penalties for violations, including fines and imprisonment. This bold move has been praised for its effectiveness in reducing plastic waste and encouraging the use of sustainable alternatives. Kenya's ban has served as a model for other African nations, many of which have followed suit with their own regulations to curb plastic bag use.

The European Union (EU) has also been proactive in addressing plastic waste. In 2019, the European Parliament adopted the Single-Use Plastics Directive, which aims to reduce the environmental impact of single-use plastics by 2021. The directive bans the use of certain single-use plastic items, such as plastic cutlery, plates, straws, and cotton buds, and sets ambitious recycling targets for plastic bottles. EU member states are required to implement these measures into their national legislation, leading to widespread changes across Europe. The EU's approach not only targets plastic items that are frequently found in marine litter but also encourages the development of alternatives and the promotion of a circular economy.

Countries across Asia have also introduced various single-use plastic bans. For instance, India has announced plans to eliminate single-use plastics by 2022 as part of its broader environmental strategy. The government has focused on plastic bags, which are widely used and difficult to recycle, but the ban is set to expand to other products in the coming years. Additionally, China, one of the world's largest producers and consumers of plastic, has implemented a ban on single-use plastic bags in major cities and announced plans to phase out other single-use plastic products by 2025. These efforts in Asia reflect the increasing recognition of the dangers posed by plastic pollution, particularly in urban environments with limited waste management infrastructure.

In North America, the United States has seen a patchwork approach to single-use plastic bans, with individual states and cities implementing their own regulations. California became the first state in the U.S. to ban single-use plastic bags in 2014, and since then, many cities, including New York City and San Francisco, have introduced bans or levies on plastic bags and straws. At the federal level, however, progress has been slow, with no national ban on single-use plastics. The lack of federal action has led to inconsistent policies across the country, making it challenging to tackle the problem on a larger scale.

EPR Laws

While single-use plastic bans are a critical step, they do not address the root cause of plastic waste: the production of plastic products. To tackle this issue, many countries have implemented EPR laws, which require producers to take responsibility for the entire life cycle of their products, including post-consumer waste. EPR laws shift the burden of waste management from governments and taxpayers to producers, encouraging businesses to design products that are easier to recycle and to take greater responsibility for the waste generated by their products.

France is one of the leaders in implementing EPR laws. In 2007, France introduced the Polluter Pays Principle in its environmental policy, which laid the groundwork for EPR laws in the country. Under the EPR framework, manufacturers of plastic products are required to finance the collection, recycling, and disposal of their products at the end of their life cycle. The French system has been highly successful in encouraging companies to reduce plastic packaging and use more sustainable materials. EPR has also provided a significant boost to recycling rates, ensuring that plastics are processed and reused rather than ending up in landfills.

In Germany, the Packaging Act, which came into force in 2019, expanded the country's existing EPR system to include more types of packaging. Under this law, producers must register with a national database, report on the amount of packaging they place on the market, and contribute to the cost of waste collection and recycling. Germany's system is regarded as one of the most effective EPR models in the world, with high recycling rates and a clear incentive structure for producers to reduce packaging waste.

Canada has also adopted EPR laws at the provincial level, particularly in British Columbia and Ontario, where producers are required to fund and manage the recycling of packaging and printed materials. These laws aim to encourage businesses to minimize plastic packaging and improve recycling infrastructure. In British Columbia, the EPR program covers a broad range of products, including household packaging, electronics, and tires, helping to reduce the amount of waste sent to landfills.

EPR laws not only incentivize companies to produce less plastic waste but also contribute to the creation of more efficient recycling systems. They have been shown to improve the quality of recycled materials and reduce the costs of recycling by shifting financial responsibility to the producers who create the waste. By encouraging companies to take responsibility for their products throughout their entire life cycle, EPR laws create a more sustainable and circular approach to managing plastic waste.

Waste Management Systems Around the World

As the global plastic waste crisis continues to escalate, efficient waste management systems are becoming increasingly critical in mitigating environmental damage and reducing pollution. Waste management strategies vary significantly across countries and regions, influenced by factors such as economic development, population density, and local infrastructure. This section explores some successful waste management systems from around the world, highlighting case studies that have made notable strides in addressing plastic waste. It also examines the roles of recycling, composting, and waste-to-energy technologies as part of the solution to plastic waste.

Case Studies of Successful Waste Management Strategies

One of the most notable examples of a successful waste management system is Sweden's approach, which has earned it international recognition for its innovation and efficiency. Sweden has developed a comprehensive waste management strategy that includes an effective combination of recycling, waste-to-energy, and waste minimization. The country recycles nearly 99% of its waste, with a particular focus on separating plastics, paper, and metals. Sweden's waste management system relies on a highly organized collection infrastructure, where waste is sorted by consumers and then processed at various facilities for recycling or energy recovery.

In addition to its recycling efforts, Sweden has implemented an innovative waste-to-energy (WtE) system, where non-recyclable waste is burned in specialized plants to generate electricity and heat. Sweden has built a network of advanced incinerators that convert waste into energy, reducing the reliance on landfills and providing a renewable energy source for the country's homes and businesses. Remarkably, Sweden imports waste from neighboring countries, such as Norway and the UK, to fuel its incinerators, further demonstrating the success of its waste management model.

Sweden's success is due in large part to its well-established waste management policies, public awareness campaigns, and a robust recycling culture. By integrating waste management into daily life, ensuring the proper separation of recyclables, and developing cutting-edge technology, Sweden has positioned itself as a global leader in sustainable waste management. Its model demonstrates the importance of combining recycling and waste-to-energy technologies while reducing the amount of waste sent to landfills.

Another success story comes from South Korea, which has transformed its waste management system through the introduction of a pay-as-you-throw (PAYT) program. This initiative encourages citizens to dispose of waste responsibly by charging fees based on the amount of waste they generate. As a result, South Korea has significantly reduced its overall waste generation, with a notable increase in recycling rates. The country also implemented a highly organized waste collection system that includes the separation of organic waste for composting and the proper sorting of recyclable materials, such as plastics, metals, and paper. In addition, South Korea has invested in building state-of-the-art recycling facilities that process large volumes of waste and recover valuable materials.

The impact of South Korea's waste management policies has been significant. The country now has one of the highest recycling rates in the world, with more than 53% of its waste being recycled. The PAYT system, along with public education campaigns about waste reduction, has helped to foster a culture of sustainability in South Korean society. This case study shows how an incentive-based approach, combined with robust infrastructure and education, can effectively manage plastic waste and reduce landfill use.

In Japan, another advanced waste management system has emerged, driven by strict policies and a culture of responsibility towards waste. Japan's waste management system focuses on source separation, where residents are required to separate their waste into categories such as burnable, non-burnable, and recyclable. The country also places significant emphasis on waste minimization through product design and packaging regulation, limiting the amount of packaging materials used by manufacturers. Public awareness programs and municipal-level recycling efforts are integral to Japan's success.

Japan has implemented sophisticated recycling technologies, including advanced sorting systems that separate different types of plastics for recycling. In addition, Japan's waste-to-energy systems have been highly successful in converting residual waste into energy, which reduces the need for landfills and provides a renewable energy source. This efficient system of waste collection, sorting, recycling, and energy recovery has allowed Japan to maintain a low landfill rate and significantly reduce plastic waste.

The Role of Recycling, Composting, and Waste-to-Energy Technologies

Recycling is one of the most critical components of an effective waste management system, as it reduces the need for new raw materials and diverts waste from landfills. Advanced recycling systems have been developed around the world to separate different types of plastics and other materials to be processed into new products. In many countries, including Sweden and South Korea, the introduction of automated sorting technology has greatly improved the efficiency of recycling systems. These systems use a combination of conveyor belts, air jets, and magnetic fields to separate recyclables, making it easier to process large volumes of waste. Once sorted, materials like plastic, glass, and metal are sent to specialized recycling plants where they can be reused in manufacturing processes.

However, while recycling is essential, it is not always sufficient on its own to address the growing plastic waste crisis. Composting is another important method of waste management, particularly for organic materials such as food waste and yard trimmings. In countries like South Korea and Japan, composting is integrated into waste management systems, allowing for the recycling of organic waste into valuable soil fertilizers. Composting reduces the amount of waste sent to landfills, decreases methane emissions from organic waste decomposition, and enriches the soil, promoting sustainable agriculture.

Finally, WtE technologies are playing an increasingly important role in managing non-recyclable waste. WtE involves the incineration of waste to generate electricity and heat, which can then be used to power homes and businesses. Countries such as Sweden and Japan have invested heavily in WtE technologies, which not only reduce the volume of waste but also provide a renewable energy source. While WtE technologies can be controversial due to concerns about air pollution and the emissions produced during incineration, modern WtE plants are equipped with advanced filtration systems that minimize environmental impact.

In addition to traditional WtE technologies, newer innovations, such as chemical recycling and biodegradable plastic alternatives, hold promise for reducing plastic waste. These technologies offer new ways to process plastics that are typically difficult to recycle, further advancing the shift toward a circular economy.

Challenges in Policy Implementation

While global and national policies to combat plastic pollution have made significant strides, numerous challenges remain in effectively implementing these policies on a large scale. These challenges include issues with enforcement, political resistance, inconsistent policies across regions, and the inherent complexities of the plastic supply chain. These obstacles complicate the goal of reducing plastic waste and require concerted efforts from governments, businesses, and civil society to overcome.

Lack of Enforcement

One of the primary barriers to effective policy implementation is the lack of enforcement of existing regulations. While many countries have introduced plastic bans, recycling initiatives, and waste management policies, the practical enforcement of these laws often proves difficult. In many regions, especially in low- and middle-income countries, the infrastructure required to manage waste and implement regulations is inadequate. For example, plastic waste disposal systems may be underfunded or poorly maintained, making it difficult to ensure that policies are being followed. Even where bans on single-use plastics exist, illegal production and sale of these products often continue unchecked due to insufficient monitoring and penalties.

In some countries, the enforcement of plastic bans or recycling regulations is hampered by corruption or a lack of political will. Local authorities, particularly in urban areas with large informal economies, may lack the resources or incentive to enforce regulations consistently. In such cases, consumers and businesses may continue to use or improperly dispose of plastic products without fear of penalty. In fact, the enforcement of plastic policies can often be seen as a low priority compared to other pressing issues, such as poverty alleviation, economic growth, and public health.

Even when enforcement mechanisms are in place, the lack of awareness and understanding about the laws among local populations can hinder compliance. In many parts of the world, people may not fully grasp the environmental consequences of plastic waste or the requirements of new waste management systems. Without proper education and outreach efforts, enforcement becomes more difficult, and policy goals are less likely to be achieved.

Political Resistance

Political resistance is another significant challenge that impedes the effective implementation of plastic waste policies. Many governments, especially in developing nations, face political and economic pressure from the plastic production industry, which is often a significant source of employment and tax revenue. In countries where plastics are a central part of the economy, any policy that seeks to reduce plastic production or consumption may face strong opposition from industry stakeholders, who argue that such policies could harm economic growth or lead to job losses. This resistance can manifest in the form of lobbying, campaign contributions, and efforts to influence policy makers at local, national, and international levels.

In some cases, industries argue that plastic products are essential for economic development, particularly in sectors like packaging, manufacturing, and agriculture. Governments may be reluctant to pass stringent plastic regulations due to concerns over negative economic impacts, particularly in the short term. As a result, plastic production and use may continue unabated, with limited regulatory oversight, which slows down progress in reducing plastic waste.

Political resistance can also arise due to partisan divides over environmental policy. In countries where environmental issues are highly politicized, there may be disagreements over the role of government in regulating plastic waste and pollution. This can lead to policy gridlock, where proposals to ban plastics or introduce recycling programs are delayed or rejected, even if they have broad public support. The difficulty in achieving political consensus on plastic waste management can lead to fragmented, inconsistent, and incomplete policy implementation across regions and countries.

Inconsistent Policies Across Regions

A major challenge in combating plastic pollution is the inconsistent implementation of policies across different regions and countries. While some nations have adopted robust policies and regulations to manage plastic waste, others have either failed to do so or have adopted policies that are less comprehensive. For example, European Union countries are generally leaders in plastic waste management, with policies like the Single-Use Plastics Directive and high recycling rates. In contrast, many low- and middle-income countries, particularly in sub-Saharan Africa and South Asia, have weaker waste management systems and less comprehensive regulatory frameworks. These regions often lack the infrastructure to properly collect, sort, and recycle plastic waste, leading to large quantities of plastic ending up in landfills or the environment.

Even within countries, policies can vary dramatically between regions. In federal systems, such as those in India, the United States, and Brazil, individual states or provinces may have their own plastic waste regulations, which can differ widely in scope and enforcement. In some regions, policies may be more stringent and effective, while others may not have the political will or resources to implement them properly. This disparity in policy implementation can lead to uneven progress in addressing plastic pollution, with some areas making significant strides while others lag behind.

The lack of harmonization in international plastic waste regulations is also a challenge. In the absence of a binding global agreement, countries have adopted differing policies, making it difficult to address plastic pollution on a global scale. For example, while some countries have adopted EPR laws, which require manufacturers to take responsibility for the collection and recycling of their products, others have not. This lack of uniformity in policy can create loopholes, allowing companies to avoid the environmental responsibilities imposed by EPR laws or other regulations.

Addressing the Complexities of the Plastic Supply Chain

Another significant challenge in implementing effective plastic waste management policies is the complexity of the plastic supply chain. Plastics are not a single product, but rather a family of materials made from various polymers that serve a multitude of applications. This complexity means that addressing plastic waste requires a multi-faceted approach that includes managing the entire plastic life cycle—from production and design to recycling and disposal.

The global nature of the plastic supply chain makes it difficult to control. Plastic products are often manufactured in one country, used in another, and disposed of in yet another. Multinational companies that produce plastic goods may operate in multiple jurisdictions with differing regulations, making it difficult to enforce waste management and recycling standards across the entire supply chain. In some cases, companies may shift production to countries with less stringent environmental regulations, creating "pollution havens" where plastic waste management is less regulated.

Moreover, plastic packaging and products are often designed without consideration for recycling. Many plastic items are made from mixed materials or contain additives that make them difficult to recycle. In addition, the vast variety of plastic products on the market makes it challenging for recycling systems to efficiently process all types of plastic waste. As a result, a large percentage of plastic waste is not recycled and ends up in landfills or the environment.

Addressing the plastic supply chain requires international cooperation to harmonize regulations, improve product design for recyclability, and create global standards for plastic waste management. The transition to a circular economy, in which plastics are reused, remanufactured, and recycled, will require the redesign of the entire plastic production and consumption system, from material sourcing to end-of-life management.

Chapter 3: The Role of Industry in Plastic Waste

Chapter 3 delves into the critical role that industries play in the plastic waste crisis, focusing on the plastic production sector, the packaging and consumer goods industries, and the growing pressure for businesses to adopt more sustainable practices. While plastic products have become indispensable in modern life, the industries responsible for their production and distribution must also take responsibility for their environmental impact. This chapter examines how these sectors contribute to plastic waste generation, the rise of corporate sustainability initiatives, and the challenges of greenwashing. Additionally, it explores innovations in packaging and product design, such as biodegradable plastics and plant-based alternatives, as businesses seek to balance profitability with environmental responsibility. Through this exploration, we highlight the urgent need for industry-wide changes to reduce plastic waste and promote a more circular economy.

Plastic Production Industry

The plastic production industry is a critical player in the global plastic waste crisis, as it is responsible for the creation of plastic products that flood the market, from packaging and household items to automotive parts and medical devices. The major corporations within this industry hold significant influence, shaping both production practices and environmental policies. However, the industry's focus on fossil fuel-based plastic production has led to substantial environmental impacts, contributing to pollution, climate change, and unsustainable resource use. This section explores the role of major corporations in the plastic production industry, their influence on plastic consumption, and the environmental challenges posed by fossil fuel-based plastic production.

Major Corporations and Their Influence on the Plastic Industry

The plastic production industry is dominated by a small number of large multinational corporations that hold significant control over global plastic production. These companies include some of the biggest players in the oil and chemical industries, such as ExxonMobil, Dow Chemical, BASF, SABIC, and Chevron Phillips Chemical. Together, these corporations account for a substantial portion of global plastic production, with some of them producing millions of tons of plastic each year. The products manufactured by these companies range from everyday consumer goods to high-tech industrial applications, all of which contribute to the growing problem of plastic waste.

These major corporations exert considerable influence over the plastic industry through their control of the supply chain. From raw material extraction to production, distribution, and disposal, these companies play a pivotal role in determining how plastic is made, how it is used, and how it is discarded. For example, ExxonMobil, one of the world's largest oil and gas companies, is also one of the largest producers of polyethylene, the most widely used plastic in the world. Similarly, Dow Chemical is a key producer of polystyrene, polypropylene, and other types of plastic used in packaging, consumer goods, and industrial applications.

As major producers of plastic, these corporations shape global demand and consumption patterns. Through aggressive marketing campaigns and widespread distribution networks, they have helped make plastic a ubiquitous material in nearly every aspect of modern life. Plastics are favored for their versatility, low cost, and convenience, which has led to their widespread adoption across industries. This dominance has made it difficult for alternatives to gain traction, as the economic benefits of plastic production are deeply entrenched in global supply chains.

However, the influence of these corporations extends beyond product manufacturing. These companies also wield significant power in shaping environmental policy and regulations related to plastic waste. Many of the largest plastic producers are involved in lobbying efforts aimed at resisting policies that could limit plastic production or impose stricter regulations on plastic waste management. For instance, some plastic producers have actively lobbied against plastic bag bans and have sought to weaken recycling regulations. Their influence has contributed to slow policy progress, particularly in countries where plastic production is a key economic driver.

The Push Towards Fossil Fuel-Based Plastic Production and Its Environmental Impact

The vast majority of plastics produced today are derived from fossil fuels, primarily petroleum and natural gas. These raw materials undergo a series of chemical processes to create plastic polymers, which are then molded and shaped into the final products. The reliance on fossil fuels for plastic production has significant environmental consequences at every stage of the process, from extraction to disposal.

Petroleum and natural gas are extracted through oil drilling and gas mining operations, both of which contribute to environmental degradation. The extraction of fossil fuels is energy-intensive and often involves practices that can harm ecosystems, such as hydraulic fracturing (fracking) and offshore drilling. These activities can result in habitat destruction, water contamination, and air pollution, all of which contribute to broader environmental problems such as climate change.

Once extracted, the petroleum and natural gas are refined into chemical feedstocks, which are then converted into plastic through processes such as polymerization. This process requires significant energy input, and the use of fossil fuels in plastic production is a major contributor to greenhouse gas emissions. In fact, the production of plastic is responsible for a substantial share of global carbon emissions, with estimates suggesting that the plastic industry accounts for nearly 4-8% of global oil consumption and up to 6% of global carbon emissions. This environmental footprint is largely due to the energy-intensive nature of plastic production, which relies on the combustion of fossil fuels to power manufacturing facilities.

The widespread use of fossil fuel-based plastics also contributes to climate change. Plastics, when produced, have a high carbon footprint, and their widespread use leads to an increase in demand for petroleum and natural gas, both of which are major contributors to global warming. Additionally, when plastic products are discarded and begin to break down in the environment, they contribute to the release of toxic substances such as dioxins, which are harmful to both the environment and human health.

Plastic products that are not recycled and end up in landfills or the natural environment can persist for hundreds of years, contributing to the accumulation of plastic waste and the formation of plastic pollution hotspots like the Great Pacific Garbage Patch. As plastics break down, they release microplastics, tiny particles that infiltrate ecosystems, waterways, and oceans, further complicating the environmental challenges associated with plastic waste.

The environmental impact of plastic production is compounded by the lack of recycling. Although some plastics are recyclable, a large portion of plastic products are not designed with recycling in mind, and many types of plastic are difficult or impossible to recycle. As a result, most of the plastic produced in the world ends up in landfills or the natural environment, exacerbating the pollution problem. The low recycling rates and limited infrastructure for plastic waste management mean that much of the plastic produced is wasted, further burdening the environment.

Alternative Materials and the Shift Toward Sustainable Production

In response to growing environmental concerns, there has been increasing pressure on plastic producers to shift away from fossil fuel-based plastics and explore sustainable alternatives. Companies are beginning to invest in bio-based plastics made from renewable resources, such as corn starch, sugarcane, or algae. These materials, often marketed as bioplastics, are seen as a potential solution to the environmental issues associated with fossil fuel-based plastics. However, challenges remain in terms of production scalability, cost-effectiveness, and the full life cycle impact of bio-based plastics, which still require energy for production and can contribute to waste if not properly managed.

Additionally, the rise of the circular economy has prompted calls for manufacturers to design plastics that are more easily recyclable or reusable, creating a closed-loop system that reduces the need for virgin materials and minimizes waste. Yet, achieving a truly circular economy for plastics remains elusive, as the current infrastructure for recycling and waste management is often insufficient to handle the vast volume of plastic waste generated globally.

The Role of Packaging and Consumer Goods

The packaging and consumer goods industries are among the largest contributors to global plastic waste, particularly in the form of single-use plastics. These industries rely heavily on plastic materials for packaging products, from food and beverages to household items and electronics. The prevalence of single-use plastics—items designed to be used once and then discarded—has contributed significantly to the growing plastic waste crisis. However, increasing awareness of the environmental impact of plastic waste has sparked innovation within these industries, leading to the development of alternatives to conventional plastic packaging. This section explores the role of packaging and consumer goods in plastic waste generation and examines the potential for alternative materials to reduce plastic consumption and waste.

Single-Use Plastics in Packaging and Retail Industries

The packaging and retail industries are among the largest consumers of single-use plastics. Plastic packaging is used extensively because of its versatility, low cost, and durability, making it an attractive option for manufacturers. Items such as plastic bags, bottles, straws, food wrappers, and packaging materials are integral to the packaging process in industries ranging from food and beverage to cosmetics, electronics, and personal care products. These single-use plastic products serve several purposes: they protect products from contamination, improve shelf life, and provide convenience for consumers. However, the widespread use of single-use plastics has led to significant environmental concerns, as most of these products are not recycled and end up in landfills or the natural environment.

Plastic packaging is used extensively in the food and beverage industry, where it is primarily employed for beverages, snacks, and packaged meals. The convenience of plastic packaging has made it the go-to material for products such as bottled drinks, ready-to-eat meals, and snack foods. For instance, plastic bottles are widely used for beverages like water, soda, and juices, while plastic containers are used for storing perishable foods like dairy products, fruits, and vegetables. According to estimates, plastic packaging accounts for around 40% of global plastic production, and a large portion of this is used in food and beverage packaging. However, much of this plastic packaging is used only briefly, with products being consumed and packaging discarded, leading to a massive volume of plastic waste.

The retail industry also plays a significant role in the proliferation of single-use plastics. Retail stores and supermarkets frequently use plastic bags, plastic wrap, and shrink wrap to package products for sale. Plastic bags are one of the most ubiquitous forms of single-use plastic, often given out in large quantities at checkouts. Despite growing efforts to reduce plastic bag usage through bans and fees in some regions, plastic bags remain a significant contributor to plastic waste. Retailers also use plastic packaging for a wide range of products, including clothing, electronics, and household items. The ease with which plastic packaging can be produced and customized for different products has made it a staple in the retail sector.

Cosmetics and personal care products represent another area of the consumer goods industry where plastic packaging is dominant. Products like shampoo bottles, toothpaste tubes, deodorants, and cosmetic containers are primarily made of plastic. These items are often single-use, with consumers using the product and then discarding the packaging. Many of these products, despite being recyclable, are not properly disposed of or recycled, adding to the growing plastic waste issue.

The use of single-use plastics in packaging creates a complex problem for waste management. While plastic products are lightweight and durable, they often cannot be easily recycled due to contamination or the materials' complexity. As a result, much of the plastic packaging used in the consumer goods and retail industries ends up in landfills or the environment, contributing to the accumulation of plastic waste and plastic pollution in natural ecosystems.

Alternatives to Conventional Plastic Packaging

In response to the growing environmental concerns about plastic waste, there has been increasing interest in developing alternatives to conventional plastic packaging. Many companies within the packaging and consumer goods sectors are seeking out sustainable solutions that can reduce the environmental footprint of their products. These alternatives range from biodegradable plastics to plant-based materials, edible packaging, and reusable containers. While no single solution is perfect, these alternatives represent a promising shift towards more sustainable practices within the industry.

Biodegradable plastics are one of the most discussed alternatives to conventional plastic packaging. Unlike traditional plastics, which can take hundreds of years to decompose, biodegradable plastics are designed to break down more quickly in the environment. Materials like polylactic acid (PLA), made from renewable resources such as corn starch or sugarcane, are becoming increasingly popular as substitutes for traditional plastic in packaging. However, biodegradable plastics face challenges, including the need for proper industrial composting facilities to break them down efficiently. If these plastics end up in landfills or the ocean, they may not degrade as intended, raising concerns about their effectiveness as an environmental solution.

Plant-based materials are another alternative to fossil fuel-derived plastics. Materials such as paper, cardboard, bamboo, and hemp are increasingly being used for packaging products, particularly in the food and beverage industry. These materials are renewable, compostable, and can be produced with a lower environmental footprint compared to plastic. For example, bamboo packaging is becoming a popular alternative for products like toothbrushes, straws, and packaging for electronics. While plant-based materials can offer significant environmental benefits, they also face challenges, such as durability and cost, which can make them less viable for certain applications compared to plastic.

Edible packaging is a more innovative solution that has gained attention in recent years. Made from ingredients such as seaweed, rice, and gelatin, edible packaging can be consumed along with the product it contains, eliminating the need for disposal. For example, edible seaweed-based wrappers are being used to package snacks and condiments. This type of packaging offers a novel approach to reducing waste, but its practicality on a larger scale remains to be seen, particularly for products with longer shelf lives or complex packaging needs.

Reusable containers represent another promising alternative to single-use plastics. Reusable packaging, such as glass or metal containers, can be used multiple times, reducing the need for disposable packaging altogether. The growing popularity of refillable water bottles, coffee cups, and food containers in the consumer market reflects a shift toward sustainability. Many retailers and food establishments are also encouraging consumers to bring their own reusable containers to reduce packaging waste. However, the widespread adoption of reusable containers depends on changes in consumer behavior and the development of convenient systems for cleaning, refilling, and reusing packaging.

Additionally, compostable packaging made from organic materials like cornstarch, cellulose, or even mushroom fibers is gaining traction as a sustainable alternative to plastic. These materials can break down in composting facilities, contributing to a more circular approach to packaging waste.

Corporate Responsibility and Greenwashing

In recent years, corporate responsibility has become a central focus for businesses across the globe, particularly in industries that contribute significantly to environmental degradation, such as plastic production, packaging, and consumer goods. As the environmental impact of plastic waste has gained widespread attention, many companies have introduced corporate sustainability initiatives aimed at reducing their environmental footprint and addressing plastic pollution. While these initiatives reflect a growing commitment to environmental sustainability, the phenomenon of greenwashing—the practice of misleading consumers about the environmental benefits of a product or company—has also emerged as a major concern. This section explores the rise of corporate sustainability initiatives, the growing emphasis on environmental responsibility, and the ways in which greenwashing can undermine genuine efforts to reduce plastic waste.

The Rise of Corporate Sustainability Initiatives

The rise of corporate sustainability initiatives is a direct response to increasing pressure from consumers, regulators, and environmental organizations. In the past decade, businesses have been compelled to reevaluate their environmental practices, particularly in relation to plastic production, packaging, and waste. As the negative environmental impact of plastic waste has become more widely recognized, companies have been prompted to adopt sustainability practices to improve their environmental performance and align with the growing demand for eco-friendly products.

One of the most notable corporate sustainability trends is the commitment by businesses to reduce plastic packaging. Companies, particularly in the food and beverage sector, have set ambitious goals to phase out single-use plastics and switch to more sustainable alternatives. For instance, Coca-Cola, one of the world's largest producers of plastic bottles, has committed to using 100% recyclable materials in its packaging by 2025 and to reducing its overall plastic usage. Similarly, Unilever, a multinational consumer goods company, has committed to making all of its plastic packaging recyclable, reusable, or compostable by 2025. These pledges are a part of broader sustainability strategies that aim to address plastic waste while improving the circularity of materials.

In addition to reducing plastic packaging, companies are increasingly adopting recycling programs, EPR initiatives, and investing in alternative materials. Brands like Nestlé and PepsiCo are exploring innovative materials such as biodegradable plastics, plant-based packaging, and paper alternatives to reduce their reliance on petroleum-based plastics. The goal is to develop packaging that can be easily recycled or composted, thereby reducing the amount of plastic waste that ends up in landfills or the environment.

Companies are also adopting sustainable supply chain practices to ensure that their entire production process is environmentally responsible. This includes sourcing raw materials from sustainable suppliers, reducing carbon emissions, and ensuring that products are produced using energy-efficient processes. For example, Patagonia, a company known for its environmental activism, has implemented policies to ensure that its products are made from recycled materials and that its production processes adhere to strict environmental standards. Similarly, IKEA has committed to using 100% sustainable cotton and sustainable wood in its products, further emphasizing its dedication to environmental responsibility.

While these initiatives reflect a growing commitment to sustainability, they are not always as effective as they may seem. The complexity of implementing sustainability practices across vast, global supply chains, coupled with a lack of transparency, has led to the rise of greenwashing—a practice that can undermine the legitimacy of corporate sustainability efforts.

Examining "Greenwashing" and Its Role in Obscuring True Environmental Responsibility

Greenwashing refers to the practice of companies portraying their products or practices as more environmentally friendly than they actually are. This often involves using misleading marketing tactics, such as vague claims about sustainability, unverified certifications, or deceptive imagery, to give the impression of environmental responsibility. Greenwashing can make it difficult for consumers to distinguish between companies that are genuinely committed to sustainability and those that are merely capitalizing on the growing demand for eco-friendly products.

One of the most common forms of greenwashing in the context of plastic waste is the use of vague or misleading claims about packaging or products. For example, some companies label their products as "eco-friendly" or "sustainable" without providing clear information about how their products are made or how they contribute to reducing plastic waste. This can lead consumers to believe they are making environmentally conscious choices when, in reality, the products may still rely on plastic packaging or unsustainable materials.

In some cases, companies may use unverified or non-credible environmental certifications to promote their products. For example, a company might label its product as "biodegradable" without providing proof that the material will break down in real-world conditions, or it may use a certification that is not recognized by credible environmental organizations. These deceptive practices exploit the consumer desire for environmentally responsible products while obscuring the lack of genuine efforts to reduce plastic waste or improve sustainability.

Marketing tactics that focus on "green" imagery are another common form of greenwashing. Companies often use imagery of nature, such as leaves or oceans, to suggest that their products are environmentally friendly, even when the product itself has little to no actual environmental benefit. This type of visual greenwashing misleads consumers into thinking they are supporting an environmentally responsible company without requiring them to critically examine the actual impact of the product.

Greenwashing is particularly problematic because it undermines the credibility of real sustainability efforts and can confuse consumers who want to make more environmentally responsible choices. When companies use deceptive tactics to appear more eco-friendly than they are, it creates an environment where consumers may lose trust in sustainability claims altogether. This erodes public confidence in the ability of companies to address plastic pollution and may ultimately discourage consumers from adopting more sustainable habits.

To combat greenwashing, organizations like The Greenwashing Index and The Better Business Bureau have begun to monitor and report on misleading environmental claims. Consumer advocacy groups and watchdog organizations are working to increase transparency and hold companies accountable for false advertising. Additionally, governments and regulatory bodies are beginning to take action to establish clearer guidelines for environmental claims and labeling, which will help consumers make informed choices and encourage companies to be more transparent about their sustainability practices.

Innovations in Packaging and Product Design

The need to reduce plastic waste has spurred a wave of innovation in the packaging and product design industries. As the environmental consequences of plastic pollution become more evident, businesses and researchers are developing new materials and technologies aimed at replacing traditional plastics with more sustainable options.

These innovations include biodegradable plastics, plant-based plastics, and other alternative materials that promise to reduce the ecological impact of packaging and product manufacturing. However, despite the potential of these alternatives, there are also challenges and limitations associated with their widespread adoption. This section examines some of the key innovations in packaging and product design, as well as the potential and limitations of these alternative materials.

Biodegradable Plastics, Plant-Based Plastics, and Other Innovations

Biodegradable plastics have garnered significant attention as an alternative to traditional petroleum-based plastics. These materials are designed to break down more easily in the environment through natural processes, which could help reduce the persistence of plastic waste in landfills and the natural environment. Biodegradable plastics are typically made from renewable resources, such as plant starches, PLA, or polyhydroxyalkanoates (PHA). When exposed to the right environmental conditions, these plastics can decompose much more quickly than conventional plastics, reducing the long-term environmental impact.

One of the most well-known examples of biodegradable plastics is PLA, which is derived from renewable plant resources such as corn or sugarcane. PLA is often used in food packaging, disposable cups, and cutlery. Unlike traditional plastics, which can take hundreds of years to break down, PLA can biodegrade in industrial composting facilities within a few months. However, PLA's biodegradability depends on specific conditions, such as high temperatures and the presence of moisture, which may not be present in all environments. If PLA ends up in a landfill or the ocean, it may not degrade as quickly as intended, and the plastic waste issue could persist.

Another innovative type of biodegradable plastic is PHA, a family of polymers produced by bacteria during fermentation. PHA is considered to be highly biodegradable and can break down in a variety of environments, including soil and marine ecosystems. PHA is produced from renewable biomass and can be used for a wide range of applications, from food packaging to medical products. However, the production costs of PHA remain relatively high, and scaling up production to meet global demand presents a significant challenge.

In addition to biodegradable plastics, plant-based plastics are gaining traction as more sustainable alternatives to conventional plastics. Unlike petroleum-based plastics, plant-based plastics are made from renewable resources, such as corn, sugarcane, and algae. These plastics are often touted as a more eco-friendly option because they are derived from plants that can be replenished annually, unlike fossil fuels, which take millions of years to form. Plant-based plastics can be used in many of the same applications as conventional plastics, including packaging, textiles, and automotive components.

Polyethylene (PE) and polypropylene (PP) are two of the most commonly used plastic polymers, and they can now be produced from renewable plant sources, rather than fossil fuels. These plant-based plastics offer the same functionality and durability as their petroleum-based counterparts, but with a lower carbon footprint. Additionally, bio-based polyethylene (Bio-PE) is designed to be compatible with existing recycling systems, making it a more viable alternative to traditional plastics in terms of waste management.

Another promising development is the use of algae-based plastics, which are being researched as a biodegradable alternative to petroleum-based plastics. Algae-based plastics are made from marine algae and can be produced using sustainable methods. These plastics are not only biodegradable but also come from renewable resources that do not require large amounts of land, water, or fertilizers to grow, making them an environmentally friendly option. Researchers are still exploring the scalability of algae-based plastics and the full range of applications for which they can be used, but the potential for algae to replace traditional plastics is promising.

Other innovative materials include mushroom packaging, which uses mycelium (the root structure of mushrooms) to create a biodegradable, compostable packaging material. This material can be grown into custom shapes and forms, providing a sustainable alternative to Styrofoam and other plastic packaging materials. Mushroom packaging is biodegradable, non-toxic, and produced with minimal energy inputs, making it an environmentally friendly option. However, the scalability of mushroom packaging remains a challenge, and it is not yet widely available in the market.

The Potential and Limitations of Alternative Materials

While the potential of biodegradable and plant-based plastics is promising, there are several limitations that need to be addressed before these materials can fully replace conventional plastics in widespread use. One of the primary challenges is cost. The production of biodegradable and plant-based plastics is often more expensive than the production of petroleum-based plastics, which can make these alternatives less economically viable for large-scale production. In particular, PHA and other bio-based materials require specialized production methods, which can increase costs. While advances in technology may reduce production costs over time, at present, the price of sustainable plastics remains a significant barrier to their widespread adoption.

Another limitation is performance. While plant-based plastics can offer similar properties to traditional plastics, some types of biodegradable plastics may not meet the performance standards required for certain applications. For example, biodegradable plastics like PLA may not be as durable or heat-resistant as traditional plastics, making them unsuitable for products that need to withstand high temperatures or heavy wear and tear. As a result, there may be limitations to the types of products that can be made from biodegradable or plant-based plastics, particularly in industries such as electronics, automotive, and packaging for hot or perishable goods.

The lack of proper infrastructure for composting or recycling biodegradable plastics is another significant challenge. While biodegradable plastics may break down more quickly than conventional plastics in the right conditions, these materials often require industrial composting facilities to fully decompose. Unfortunately, such facilities are not universally available, particularly in low- and middle-income countries. Without the proper infrastructure in place to handle biodegradable plastics, they may still end up in landfills or the natural environment, where they may not degrade as intended.

Furthermore, the land use required to produce bio-based plastics remains a concern. While plant-based plastics are derived from renewable resources, large-scale production of crops for bioplastics can place pressure on agricultural land, competing with food production and contributing to deforestation. The environmental impact of large-scale bio-based plastic production must be carefully considered to avoid unintended consequences, such as increased greenhouse gas emissions or environmental degradation due to intensive farming practices.

Finally, consumer education is essential in ensuring the success of alternative materials. Many consumers may not fully understand the differences between biodegradable, compostable, and recyclable plastics, leading to confusion about how to properly dispose of these materials. In some cases, biodegradable plastics may be treated as conventional plastics in waste management systems, which could undermine their environmental benefits.

Chapter 4: Plastic Waste Management and Recycling

Chapter 4 explores the essential role of plastic waste management and recycling in mitigating the global plastic pollution crisis. Effective waste management systems are crucial for addressing the vast amounts of plastic waste generated each year, and recycling plays a central role in reducing the need for new plastic production while conserving resources. This chapter delves into the current state of global plastic recycling, the various challenges associated with sorting and processing different types of plastic, and the technological innovations that are transforming the recycling landscape. It also examines the potential of alternative waste management approaches, such as waste-to-energy technologies, and explores the principles of zero-waste and circular economy models as sustainable solutions for reducing plastic waste. Ultimately, this chapter underscores the need for integrated waste management strategies that combine recycling, innovation, and global cooperation to combat plastic pollution.

Current Recycling Systems

The global state of plastic recycling is far from optimal, with significant gaps in the infrastructure, technology, and public awareness needed to effectively manage plastic waste. Despite advances in recycling systems in some parts of the world, the global recycling rate for plastics remains low, with many countries still struggling to process plastic waste efficiently. While plastics are highly versatile and can be recycled, the vast majority of plastic materials are not recycled properly, leading to substantial environmental and economic costs. This section explores the current state of plastic recycling, the challenges associated with recycling different types of plastic, and the complexities of sorting and processing plastic waste.

The Global State of Plastic Recycling

Plastic recycling has made some strides over the past few decades, with countries like Germany, Sweden, and South Korea being leaders in the field. However, on a global scale, plastic recycling rates remain disappointingly low. According to the World Economic Forum, only about 9% of plastic waste is successfully recycled worldwide, with the remainder being sent to landfills, incinerators, or ending up in the natural environment. The limited recycling rates can be attributed to several factors, including insufficient recycling infrastructure, lack of consumer participation, and technical challenges in processing certain types of plastic.

One of the main barriers to widespread plastic recycling is the lack of effective collection and sorting systems. In many countries, recycling systems are poorly developed, particularly in low- and middle-income nations. For example, in parts of Africa and South Asia, plastic waste is often collected informally or left to accumulate in public spaces, with limited efforts to separate recyclable plastics from general waste. Even in high-income countries, the inconsistency of recycling programs across regions and municipalities can hinder effective plastic recycling. Different cities and regions may have different guidelines for what can be recycled, and some areas lack the infrastructure to collect and process plastics at scale.

Developed countries such as those in Europe and North America have made progress in establishing curbside recycling programs and waste management systems. In Germany, for example, the introduction of the Green Dot system in the 1990s established a nationwide recycling infrastructure where producers are responsible for ensuring that their products and packaging are recyclable. Germany boasts one of the highest plastic recycling rates in the world, recycling around 55% of its plastic packaging. Other countries, such as South Korea, have implemented PAYT systems, which incentivize households to reduce waste by charging for the amount of waste they generate, thereby encouraging recycling and waste reduction.

Despite these positive examples, global progress remains uneven. While some countries have managed to increase their recycling rates, others have failed to establish robust recycling systems, particularly in parts of Asia where plastic waste has been a significant issue. The lack of universal standards for recycling across countries further complicates the global effort to tackle plastic waste.

Types of Plastic and the Challenges of Sorting and Processing

One of the core challenges of plastic recycling is the variety of plastic types and their differing properties, which complicate the recycling process. Plastics are categorized into several types based on their chemical composition, and each type has its own characteristics, recycling methods, and limitations. The most common plastics used in packaging and consumer goods are PE, PP, polyethylene terephthalate (PET), polystyrene (PS), and polyvinyl chloride (PVC). Each of these plastics requires different processes for recycling, and not all plastics are equally recyclable.

• PET: PET is one of the most widely used plastics, found in bottles, food containers, and clothing fibers. It is generally accepted by most recycling programs and can be processed relatively easily. However, the challenge with PET is ensuring that it is properly cleaned and free from contaminants, as dirty plastics can significantly reduce the quality of the recycled material. PET is commonly recycled into products such as t-shirts, jackets, or new bottles.

• PE: PE is used in products like plastic bags, bottles, and shrink wraps. While PE is recyclable, it is often contaminated by food or other materials, which makes it harder to recycle. Low-density polyethylene (LDPE), used in plastic bags, is particularly difficult to recycle due to its flexible nature. Many curbside programs do not accept LDPE, meaning much of it ends up in landfills or the environment.

• PP: Polypropylene is used in food containers, straws, and bottle caps. It is one of the most challenging plastics to recycle, as it often requires specialized equipment to process. While some countries and regions are able to recycle PP, the plastic is not universally accepted by recycling programs. As a result, significant amounts of PP end up in the waste stream, contributing to plastic pollution.

• Polystyrene (PS): Polystyrene is used in disposable cups, plates, and packaging material. PS is difficult to recycle due to its low density and the fact that it often contains contaminants. Many recycling facilities do not accept polystyrene, and it is often disposed of through incineration or landfilling. The environmental impact of PS is significant, as it can break into small particles that persist in the environment, particularly in marine ecosystems.

• PVC: PVC is commonly used in plumbing pipes, flooring, and bottles. Recycling PVC is challenging because it contains harmful chemicals, such as chlorine, which can release toxic fumes during processing. Additionally, PVC products are often mixed with other materials, making them difficult to sort and process. As a result, PVC recycling rates are low, and the material often ends up in landfills or is incinerated.

Sorting plastics by type is a critical first step in the recycling process. However, contamination is a significant issue. Food waste, oils, and other contaminants can prevent plastics from being properly processed, leading to lower-quality recycled products. Recycling facilities often need to clean and wash plastic items before they can be processed, adding to the cost and complexity of the recycling process. Furthermore, mixed plastics, which are often found in packaging, pose a challenge because they cannot be recycled in the same way as single-material plastics. This results in the blending of various plastic types, which can create mixed-quality products that are not as valuable or usable in manufacturing.

Additionally, plastic products designed for single use, such as straws, plastic wrap, and food containers, present challenges because they are often made from composite materials or contain additives that make recycling more difficult. As a result, many of these products are not accepted by recycling programs and end up contributing to plastic waste that cannot be easily processed or reused.

Innovations in Recycling Technology

In response to these challenges, there has been an ongoing effort to improve recycling technologies. New sorting technologies, such as automated sorting systems, are being developed to increase the efficiency and accuracy of plastic recycling. These systems use technologies like infrared spectroscopy, air jets, and robots to identify and separate different types of plastic, making it easier to process plastics that were previously difficult to sort.

Another promising area of innovation is chemical recycling, which aims to break down plastics into their molecular components so they can be repurposed into new plastic materials. Unlike mechanical recycling, which involves physically breaking down plastics, chemical recycling can process mixed plastics and complex materials. This technology is still in the early stages of development, but it holds the potential to revolutionize plastic recycling by enabling the recycling of a wider range of plastic types.

Technological Innovations in Recycling

As the global plastic waste crisis continues to grow, there has been a surge in the development and adoption of advanced recycling technologies aimed at improving plastic recycling efficiency and capacity. Traditional recycling methods, which typically involve mechanical processes to sort, shred, and melt plastic into new forms, face significant limitations due to contamination, mixed plastic types, and the decreasing quality of recycled materials. To address these challenges and significantly enhance recycling rates, researchers and companies have been exploring chemical recycling, enzymatic breakdown, and closed-loop recycling systems as more effective solutions for dealing with plastic waste. These innovations offer the promise of a more sustainable approach to managing plastic waste by expanding the types of plastics that can be recycled and reducing the environmental impact of recycling.

Advanced Recycling Methods: Chemical Recycling, Enzymatic Breakdown, and More

One of the most promising advancements in plastic recycling is chemical recycling, also known as advanced recycling. Unlike traditional recycling, which involves physically breaking down plastics into smaller pieces, chemical recycling breaks down plastics at the molecular level. This process involves using chemical reactions to de-polymerize plastics, breaking them into their original monomers or other valuable chemical products. These monomers can then be reused to create new plastic products, without the loss of material quality that occurs in mechanical recycling.

Chemical recycling can be applied to a much broader range of plastics compared to traditional methods. For example, it has the potential to recycle mixed plastics, which are often not suitable for mechanical recycling due to contamination or the presence of different plastic types. Chemical recycling processes, such as pyrolysis, gasification, and depolymerization, offer the ability to process difficult-to-recycle plastics, such as polystyrene, PVC, and multilayer packaging, which are typically excluded from traditional recycling streams.

• Pyrolysis, one of the most widely studied forms of chemical recycling, involves heating plastic waste in the absence of oxygen to break it down into valuable chemicals or fuels. Pyrolysis can recycle a wide range of plastics and turn them into liquid hydrocarbons, which can be used as feedstock for the production of new plastics or converted into synthetic fuels.

• Gasification is another promising chemical recycling method that involves converting plastics into gases, such as carbon monoxide and hydrogen, through a high-temperature reaction. These gases can be used as raw materials for creating new plastic products or generating energy.

• Depolymerization is a more targeted form of chemical recycling that breaks down specific polymers, such as PET (polyethylene terephthalate), into their original monomers. These monomers can then be purified and repolymerized into new plastic items. This process holds particular promise for recycling common plastic products, such as beverage bottles, which make up a significant portion of global plastic waste.

Enzymatic breakdown is another innovative method for recycling plastics, particularly for polyester-based plastics, such as PET. Enzymatic recycling involves using naturally occurring enzymes to break down plastics into their monomers. This process is more selective and operates at lower temperatures and pressures compared to chemical recycling, which could make it a more energy-efficient option. Recent research has led to the discovery of enzymes that can break down PET into its building blocks, which can then be used to create new, high-quality PET plastic. Enzymatic recycling holds great promise for enhancing the sustainability of PET plastic recycling, as it could significantly reduce the energy needed for plastic processing and improve the purity of the recycled material.

A notable development in enzymatic recycling is the work being done by companies like Carbios, which has developed an enzyme capable of breaking down PET plastics in a matter of hours. This breakthrough could lead to scalable, efficient recycling of PET plastics and address one of the largest plastic waste streams worldwide. Though the technology is still being refined, enzymatic recycling represents a promising step toward more efficient, lower-energy plastic recycling.

The Promise of Closed-Loop Recycling Systems

Another promising innovation in plastic recycling is the concept of closed-loop recycling systems, which aim to create a circular economy for plastic materials. In a closed-loop system, plastic products are recycled back into the same or similar products, maintaining the quality of the material throughout multiple cycles. The goal of closed-loop recycling is to minimize waste, reduce the need for virgin materials, and ensure that plastics are continually reused, rather than ending up in landfills or the environment.

The success of closed-loop recycling systems depends on several factors, including efficient sorting and collection systems, the use of high-quality recyclable plastics, and the development of advanced recycling technologies that can process a wide variety of plastics. For instance, PET bottles are one of the most commonly recycled plastics through closed-loop systems, as they can be cleaned, reprocessed, and transformed back into new bottles or other products without significant degradation in material quality. Companies like Coca-Cola and Nestlé have set ambitious goals to increase the use of recycled content in their plastic bottles, with Coca-Cola aiming for 50% recycled content in its plastic bottles by 2030.

A key component of closed-loop recycling is the use of recyclable-only packaging. Companies are increasingly designing their products with recyclability in mind, creating packaging that is easier to sort and process. Some companies have also begun to implement deposit return schemes (DRS), where consumers are incentivized to return empty bottles or cans for recycling in exchange for a refund. This system is particularly effective for PET bottles and aluminum cans, as it encourages high collection rates and ensures that the materials are returned to the recycling loop, rather than being discarded.

The development of food-grade recycled plastics is another area of focus within closed-loop recycling. Traditionally, recycled plastics were considered unsuitable for food contact due to contamination risks and the degradation of the material during recycling. However, advances in chemical recycling and purification technologies are making it possible to produce high-quality, food-safe recycled plastics. This breakthrough has the potential to close the loop on plastic packaging in the food industry, enabling companies to use recycled plastics in food packaging without sacrificing safety or quality.

One of the challenges of achieving truly closed-loop systems is the need to address plastic contamination. Contamination, often in the form of food residues, labels, or other materials, can significantly reduce the quality of the recycled material, making it unsuitable for reuse in high-quality products. However, innovations in sorting and cleaning technologies are helping to reduce contamination levels, improving the efficiency of closed-loop systems.

Challenges and Limitations of Plastic Recycling

While recycling is a vital component of waste management strategies to address the global plastic waste crisis, several challenges and limitations hinder the effectiveness of plastic recycling systems worldwide. Contamination, cost, infrastructure challenges, and low recycling rates are some of the most significant barriers to efficient plastic recycling. Despite advances in recycling technologies, these issues persist, limiting the scope of plastic recycling efforts and often rendering many plastics unrecyclable or difficult to process. This section explores the key challenges and limitations faced by the recycling industry and discusses potential solutions to improve the economics and effectiveness of plastic recycling.

Contamination, Cost, and Infrastructure Challenges

Contamination is one of the most significant barriers to successful plastic recycling. Contaminants in plastic waste—such as food residues, oils, labels, adhesives, and other materials—can interfere with the recycling process, reducing the quality and purity of the recycled material. For example, plastic containers contaminated with food or liquids may be difficult to process, as cleaning them can require additional resources, time, and energy. In some cases, plastic items that are heavily contaminated must be discarded or sent to landfills, further exacerbating the waste problem.

Contamination not only affects the quality of recycled plastics but also increases the cost and complexity of recycling. Recycling facilities must invest in specialized sorting and cleaning technologies to ensure that plastics are adequately prepared for processing. This can be a significant financial burden, particularly in countries with limited waste management resources or in regions with poorly developed recycling infrastructure. Additionally, contamination can lead to a reduction in the efficiency of recycling processes, increasing energy consumption and operational costs.

Cost is another critical factor limiting the success of plastic recycling. In many cases, recycling plastic is more expensive than producing new plastic from virgin materials. The cost of collecting, sorting, cleaning, and processing plastic waste often exceeds the value of the recycled material, making it less economically viable for companies and municipalities to recycle plastic on a large scale. This is particularly true for certain types of plastic, such as PVC and polystyrene, which are difficult and expensive to recycle due to the complexity of their chemical composition.

The high cost of recycling is compounded by the global supply chain dynamics that make virgin plastic production cheaper. Plastic production from fossil fuels benefits from economies of scale and subsidies, making it a more affordable option for manufacturers. In contrast, recycling systems—particularly those in lower-income countries—often lack the infrastructure and investment needed to make recycling processes cost-effective. The price disparity between virgin plastics and recycled plastics makes it difficult for recycled materials to compete in the marketplace, leading to a situation where many plastics are not recycled and continue to accumulate in landfills or the environment.

Infrastructure challenges further complicate the problem of plastic recycling. While some countries, particularly in Europe, have invested in robust recycling systems, many regions around the world still lack the necessary infrastructure to collect, sort, and process plastic waste effectively. In developing countries, the infrastructure for plastic waste management is often underfunded or non-existent.

Waste collection systems may be limited, and recycling facilities may be outdated, inefficient, or unable to handle the volume of plastic waste generated. This lack of infrastructure not only makes recycling difficult but also leads to a large proportion of plastic waste being mismanaged or disposed of improperly, exacerbating plastic pollution.

In many urban areas, informal waste management systems, where scavengers and waste pickers sort plastic materials by hand, are common. While this informal recycling system helps divert some plastic from landfills, it is often inefficient and lacks the capacity to process larger quantities of plastic waste. Furthermore, informal recycling operations may not have the technological means to separate and clean plastics, leading to higher contamination rates and lower-quality recycled materials.

Addressing the Low Recycling Rates and the Economics of Recycling

Despite the importance of recycling in managing plastic waste, global recycling rates remain low, with only about 9% of plastic waste being successfully recycled. This low recycling rate can be attributed to a combination of factors, including consumer behavior, lack of infrastructure, and the economic challenges associated with recycling. In many regions, plastic recycling is not a priority, and consumers may not be aware of the importance of properly sorting and disposing of plastic waste. Public education and awareness campaigns are often inadequate, leading to low participation rates in recycling programs.

Furthermore, many types of plastic are simply not recycled at all. Plastics that are made from composite materials or contain additives that make them difficult to process often end up in landfills or incinerators. For example, multi-layer packaging and plastic films are not easily recyclable due to the complexity of separating the different materials. Additionally, single-use plastics, which are designed to be used briefly and discarded, often cannot be recycled in traditional systems, contributing to the low recycling rates.

The economics of recycling play a crucial role in driving these low recycling rates. In many cases, the lack of financial incentives for recycling makes it less attractive for businesses and municipalities to invest in recycling infrastructure. For example, plastic bottle DRS in some countries, where consumers pay a deposit on bottles that is refunded when the bottles are returned for recycling, have proven to be effective in increasing recycling rates. However, implementing similar schemes for other types of plastic packaging has proven more difficult due to the higher costs involved and the complexity of recycling certain types of plastic.

In regions where the cost of recycling exceeds the value of recycled plastic materials, there is little incentive for companies to invest in recycling programs. Market demand for recycled plastics is often low, particularly in developing countries where the cost of virgin plastic production is cheaper. Furthermore, the price of recycled plastics is often volatile, depending on market conditions, which can make it an unstable and unappealing option for businesses. Until recycling becomes more economically viable and competitive with virgin plastic production, it is likely that low recycling rates will persist.

Governments can play a key role in improving the economics of recycling by implementing EPR laws, which require manufacturers to take responsibility for the collection, recycling, and disposal of their products. EPR laws shift the financial burden of waste management from taxpayers to producers, incentivizing companies to design products and packaging that are easier to recycle and ensuring that plastic waste is properly collected and processed. Additionally, governments can offer subsidies or tax incentives to support the development of recycling infrastructure and the adoption of new technologies.

Waste-to-Energy Technologies

WtE technologies have emerged as a potential solution for managing plastic and other waste materials while simultaneously recovering energy from the process. These technologies involve converting waste, including plastics, into energy in the form of electricity, heat, or biofuels, through various processes such as incineration, gasification, and anaerobic digestion. While WtE technologies can offer an effective way to reduce the volume of waste and generate renewable energy, they also come with environmental and economic trade-offs that need to be carefully considered. This section explores the various methods of energy recovery from waste, examines the associated environmental challenges, and discusses the future potential of WtE solutions in managing plastic waste.

Exploring Energy Recovery Through Incineration and Other Technologies

Incineration is one of the most widely used and well-established methods of waste-to-energy. The process involves burning waste materials, including plastics, at high temperatures in specialized furnaces or incinerators. The heat generated from the combustion process is then used to produce steam, which drives turbines to generate electricity, or the heat is captured and used directly for district heating. Incineration can significantly reduce the volume of waste by up to 90%, making it an attractive option for managing non-recyclable or difficult-to-recycle plastics.

Incineration facilities are capable of processing large amounts of waste and generating significant amounts of energy. In some regions, waste-to-energy plants contribute a substantial portion of local energy supply, especially in countries like Sweden, Denmark, and Japan, where WtE plants are integrated into the national energy grid. The energy produced from waste incineration can offset the need for fossil fuels, reducing dependence on coal, oil, and natural gas.

However, incineration has several drawbacks. The most significant concern is the emission of pollutants. Although modern incineration plants are equipped with advanced air filtration systems to minimize emissions, they still release greenhouse gases (GHGs), including carbon dioxide (CO_2), as well as potentially harmful chemicals such as dioxins, furans, and heavy metals. These substances can have harmful effects on both human health and the environment, particularly when incineration plants are not adequately controlled or maintained.

Another challenge with incineration is the high operational cost, which can make it economically unfeasible in some regions. The initial construction costs of incineration plants can be substantial, and the ongoing costs of maintaining and operating the facilities are significant. Additionally, the efficiency of energy recovery is limited by the type and composition of the waste being burned. Plastics, for example, are highly calorific, meaning they produce more energy when burned than organic waste materials, but this can also increase the emission of pollutants.

In contrast to incineration, gasification is a newer technology that converts organic and inorganic materials into a synthetic gas (syngas) through a high-temperature process in an oxygen-limited environment. The syngas can then be used to generate electricity or converted into chemicals, fuels, or biofuels. Gasification is often seen as a cleaner alternative to incineration because it produces fewer emissions and can handle a broader range of waste materials, including plastics, wood, and biomass. However, it remains a more expensive technology, and the commercialization of large-scale gasification plants has been slow.

Anaerobic digestion is another form of energy recovery, but it is primarily suited for organic waste such as food scraps and agricultural waste, rather than plastics. This process involves the breakdown of organic materials by microorganisms in the absence of oxygen, producing biogas, which can be used to generate electricity or heat. While anaerobic digestion is not typically used for plastic waste, it has gained popularity as a waste management solution for organic materials, and it can complement incineration or gasification systems in mixed waste management operations.

Environmental Trade-Offs and the Future of Waste-to-Energy Solutions

While WtE technologies provide a potential solution for plastic waste and energy recovery, they come with several environmental trade-offs that must be carefully considered. One of the primary concerns is the potential impact on air quality. As mentioned, even modern incinerators with advanced filtration systems can release pollutants into the atmosphere, including GHGs and toxic substances. Although these emissions are generally much lower than in older incinerators, the cumulative impact of many WtE facilities operating around the world could contribute significantly to global warming and local air pollution.

Another trade-off is the competition for materials between recycling and WtE. Incineration of plastics and other materials that could otherwise be recycled means that valuable resources are being lost as they are burned rather than repurposed. In a circular economy, the priority should be to reduce, reuse, and recycle materials to extend their lifecycle. Using plastics as fuel in WtE plants may seem like an attractive solution in the short term, but it diverts attention away from reducing plastic production and consumption and hinders efforts to move toward a more sustainable, closed-loop system for plastic management.

Furthermore, energy recovery from plastics through WtE is not a perfect substitute for traditional renewable energy sources such as solar, wind, or hydroelectric power. While WtE does reduce the volume of waste, it still produces energy by burning fossil-derived materials. Plastics are made from petrochemicals, and their incineration generates emissions that contribute to climate change, which runs counter to broader efforts to reduce dependence on fossil fuels and mitigate the effects of global warming. Some argue that prioritizing WtE over other forms of renewable energy production may delay the transition to cleaner, sustainable energy sources.

The future of WtE solutions will likely depend on advancements in technology and policy frameworks that ensure these systems are part of a broader waste management strategy focused on sustainability. For instance, the development of carbon capture and storage (CCS) technologies could help mitigate the emissions from WtE plants, making them a more viable option for reducing waste while generating energy. Furthermore, improved recycling infrastructure and the promotion of a circular economy, which prioritizes recycling over disposal, could reduce the amount of plastic waste that needs to be incinerated in the first place.

A sustainable waste-to-energy model will require the integration of multiple technologies and approaches, including recycling, composting, and energy recovery, to ensure that plastic waste is minimized and managed in the most environmentally responsible way. For example, by focusing on advanced sorting technologies, plastics can be better separated from other materials and directed into appropriate recycling streams, reducing the need for incineration. Moreover, governments and industry stakeholders should focus on policy incentives that promote waste prevention, the reduction of single-use plastics, and the adoption of more sustainable packaging alternatives.

Zero-Waste and Circular Economy Models

The zero-waste and circular economy models represent a transformative shift away from traditional waste management approaches, which often focus on disposal or incineration, towards more sustainable and regenerative systems. These models aim to minimize waste, reduce resource consumption, and promote the reuse and recycling of materials to create a closed-loop system. As plastic waste continues to pose significant environmental challenges, both zero-waste and circular economy models offer potential solutions for reducing plastic pollution and transitioning towards a more sustainable future. This section explores the core principles of zero-waste philosophy and examines the circular economy as a sustainable alternative to linear consumption models.

Principles of Zero-Waste Philosophy

The zero-waste philosophy is built on the idea that all materials should be reused, recycled, or composted, and that waste should be reduced to an absolute minimum. The goal is to move away from the traditional "take, make, dispose" model of production and consumption, where products are used briefly and then discarded, often ending up in landfills or incinerators. Instead, zero-waste advocates propose a more sustainable and responsible approach where the design and production of products are geared towards their reuse, repair, or recycling, and ultimately, no waste should be sent to the landfill.

The zero-waste hierarchy is a central concept in this philosophy. It prioritizes the following strategies for reducing waste:

1. Refuse: The first step in zero-waste is to refuse unnecessary items or products that cannot be reused or recycled. This involves rejecting single-use plastics and other disposable products, focusing instead on purchasing durable, long-lasting goods.

2. Reduce: The second principle emphasizes minimizing waste generation. This includes buying products with minimal packaging, reducing consumption, and opting for items that are multifunctional or can be reused multiple times.

3. Reuse: Reusing products and materials whenever possible is the third principle. This can involve repurposing containers, donating or repairing goods, and choosing products that are designed for longevity rather than short-term use.

4. Recycle: Recycling plays an important role in zero-waste, but it comes after refusing, reducing, and reusing. Properly sorting and recycling materials ensures that valuable resources are not wasted and can be turned into new products. However, recycling should be considered as a last resort after other waste reduction methods have been exhausted.

5. Rot: The final principle involves composting organic waste. This includes food scraps, yard waste, and other biodegradable materials, which can be turned into nutrient-rich compost rather than ending up in landfills.

Zero-waste philosophy advocates for a systemic change in the way society consumes and disposes of products. This philosophy encourages individuals, businesses, and governments to rethink the entire lifecycle of products, from design to disposal, and to adopt practices that prioritize sustainability and the elimination of waste. Zero-waste communities have emerged globally, where municipalities and businesses are implementing zero-waste programs to reduce the amount of waste sent to landfills. For example, cities like San Francisco and Kamikatsu in Japan have implemented zero-waste initiatives that include extensive recycling programs, composting, and a focus on reducing single-use plastics.

While zero-waste principles have made progress in many urban centers, challenges remain, particularly in industries that rely heavily on plastic packaging and disposable products. However, the zero-waste movement has gained momentum, and many businesses, including retailers and food service companies, are shifting towards practices that support the philosophy, such as offering refill stations, reducing packaging, and creating products designed for reuse.

Circular Economy as a Sustainable Alternative to Linear Consumption Models

The circular economy is a model of production and consumption that aims to keep resources in use for as long as possible, extracting maximum value from them while in use, then recovering and regenerating products and materials at the end of their service life. The circular economy contrasts sharply with the linear economy, which follows a "take, make, dispose" model, where raw materials are extracted, products are manufactured and used, and then discarded as waste. The circular economy seeks to close this loop, creating a system where waste is minimized, and products are continuously reused, refurbished, and recycled.

The core principles of the circular economy include:

1. Design for longevity: Products should be designed to be durable, repairable, and easy to disassemble. This reduces the need for frequent replacements and minimizes the amount of waste generated from discarded products. By creating goods that last longer, the circular economy reduces the need for new raw materials and minimizes waste.

2. Maintain and extend the life of products: Instead of discarding products once they have reached the end of their useful life, the circular economy encourages repair, refurbishment, and remanufacturing. By extending the life of products, valuable materials and resources are kept in circulation for longer, reducing the need to produce new items and conserving natural resources.

3. Reuse and recycling: In a circular economy, products and materials are reused or recycled to create new products, reducing the reliance on virgin raw materials. For example, plastic bottles can be collected, cleaned, and reused to make new bottles or other products. In some cases, materials can be broken down into their constituent parts and used to create new materials, reducing waste and conserving resources.

4. Regenerative processes: The circular economy also focuses on regenerative processes that restore or enhance natural systems. This includes practices such as composting organic waste, which returns nutrients to the soil, and using renewable energy sources to power production processes. By prioritizing regenerative practices, the circular economy ensures that resources are replenished rather than depleted.

The circular economy is often referred to as a system of "closed-loop" production, where materials continuously flow through the system, with minimal loss or waste. This approach reduces the need for landfill disposal and minimizes the environmental impact of plastic production and waste. For instance, closed-loop recycling systems, such as those used for PET bottles, aim to continuously recycle plastic into new plastic bottles without degradation in material quality. Companies like Coca-Cola and Unilever are increasingly adopting circular economy practices, with goals to make their packaging recyclable and use recycled materials in their products.

One of the key challenges in implementing the circular economy is the design of products for recyclability and reuse. Many products, especially plastics, are difficult to recycle because they contain mixed materials or additives that complicate processing. To overcome this, companies must design products that are easily separable, reusable, or recyclable without the need for complex processes. For example, product packaging could be made from a single material, eliminating the need for complicated sorting and processing systems.

Additionally, transitioning from a linear to a circular economy requires changes in consumer behavior. Consumers must be educated about the benefits of recycling and reuse, and they must be incentivized to participate in circular systems, such as returning used products for recycling or repair. Governments also have a role to play in creating policies that support circular economy practices, such as offering incentives for businesses to adopt sustainable practices and implementing regulations that reduce waste.

Chapter 5: Pathways to Reducing Plastic Waste

Chapter 5 explores various pathways to reducing plastic waste, focusing on the multifaceted approaches needed to tackle the global plastic waste crisis. This chapter examines key strategies, including behavioral change and consumer awareness, the development of alternative materials, and the increasing role of corporate responsibility and innovation. It also highlights the importance of policy and legal solutions in driving systemic change. By delving into these pathways, the chapter aims to provide practical solutions and actionable steps that can help reduce plastic waste across all levels—individual, industry, and government—ultimately contributing to a more sustainable, plastic-free future.

Behavioral Change and Consumer Awareness

One of the most significant challenges in tackling the global plastic waste crisis is the behavior of consumers. The way individuals perceive, use, and dispose of plastic products directly impacts the amount of waste generated and the effectiveness of recycling systems. Changing consumer behavior and fostering greater awareness of the environmental impacts of plastic are essential components of any strategy to reduce plastic waste. In this context, both individual action and grassroots movements play a crucial role, while education and public awareness campaigns can drive the broader societal shifts needed to reduce plastic consumption and improve waste management practices. This section explores the power of behavioral change, grassroots movements, and the role of education in raising consumer awareness about plastic waste.

The Power of Individual Action and Grassroots Movements

At the core of reducing plastic waste is the empowerment of individuals to make sustainable choices. While systemic changes and industry-level actions are crucial, individual actions also have a significant impact. Consumer choices influence demand for plastic products, and shifting those choices toward sustainable alternatives can create a ripple effect, encouraging businesses and governments to adopt more environmentally friendly practices.

Individual action can take many forms, from reducing plastic consumption to actively participating in recycling programs. Simple lifestyle changes, such as opting for reusable bags, water bottles, and containers, can significantly reduce plastic waste. Plastic-free shopping initiatives are becoming increasingly popular, with consumers choosing products with minimal or no plastic packaging. Similarly, individuals can choose products made from more sustainable materials, such as biodegradable packaging or plant-based plastics. By avoiding single-use plastics, individuals not only reduce the waste they generate but also send a clear signal to businesses that there is a growing demand for sustainable alternatives.

The power of grassroots movements in fostering behavioral change cannot be underestimated. These movements, which often start at the community level, seek to raise awareness about the environmental impact of plastic waste and encourage individuals to take action. Grassroots efforts can be seen in various campaigns and initiatives aimed at reducing plastic waste, such as local beach clean-ups, plastic-free challenges, and community recycling programs. These efforts not only encourage individuals to reduce their plastic use but also help build a collective sense of responsibility for environmental stewardship.

In many cases, grassroots movements can inspire large-scale change by influencing public opinion and putting pressure on governments and businesses to act. For example, the plastic bag ban movement, which started with local advocacy and consumer demand, has now been adopted by many countries and cities around the world. Similarly, local initiatives such as Plastic Free July, which encourages individuals to commit to going without plastic for an entire month, have grown into global campaigns that inspire millions of people to rethink their plastic consumption habits.

Grassroots movements are particularly effective at reaching communities that may not be engaged by large corporations or government initiatives. These movements foster a sense of ownership and involvement, encouraging participants to become ambassadors for change within their own social networks. As these movements grow and gain traction, they create a broader culture of environmental consciousness, which can ultimately lead to larger, more systemic changes.

Education and Public Awareness Campaigns

While individual actions and grassroots movements are essential, widespread change requires education and public awareness campaigns to inform the broader population about the environmental impact of plastic waste and the need for behavioral change. Education can help individuals understand the consequences of their plastic consumption, the limitations of current recycling systems, and the importance of reducing plastic waste.

Public awareness campaigns have played a key role in raising awareness about plastic pollution and the environmental threats it poses. The global success of campaigns like "Say No to Plastic", "Break Free From Plastic", and "Plastic Pollution Coalition" has helped shine a spotlight on the dangers of plastic waste, particularly in the ocean, where millions of tons of plastic debris accumulate each year. These campaigns highlight the impact of plastic on wildlife, ecosystems, and human health, serving as powerful tools for inspiring individuals to take action.

One of the most successful approaches to public awareness has been the visual impact of plastic waste. Documentaries like "Plastic Oceans" and "A Plastic Planet" have shown the stark reality of plastic pollution, from the massive floating garbage patches in the ocean to the microplastics found in marine life. These visual representations of the problem serve to awaken public consciousness and catalyze action. By using emotional storytelling and highlighting the interconnectedness of human and environmental health, these campaigns have effectively communicated the urgency of addressing plastic waste.

Education is also essential in informing people about recycling and the limitations of current systems. Many consumers are unaware of the complexities of plastic recycling, which can lead to contamination of recycling streams and the inefficiency of recycling programs. By educating the public on proper sorting techniques and the types of plastics that can be recycled, recycling rates can be improved. This information is especially crucial in communities where recycling systems are in place but are underutilized due to lack of awareness or confusion about the rules.

Schools, local governments, and non-governmental organizations (NGOs) are critical in educating young people about the importance of reducing plastic waste. Educational programs focused on sustainability, environmental stewardship, and waste management can have long-term effects by instilling eco-friendly habits early on. Schools can incorporate lessons on the importance of recycling and reducing plastic consumption into their curricula, while also engaging students in hands-on activities like organizing clean-ups and participating in sustainability projects. As the next generation grows up with these values, they are more likely to adopt sustainable practices and encourage their families and communities to do the same.

Governments and businesses also have a role to play in educating consumers about the environmental impact of plastic waste. Governments can use advertising and social media campaigns to promote awareness of plastic waste issues and encourage individuals to take steps to reduce plastic consumption. For instance, campaigns that promote reusable shopping bags or water bottles can be coupled with educational messages about the environmental cost of plastic production and disposal. Similarly, businesses can help by labeling their products with clear recycling instructions and information about the environmental impact of their packaging.

In addition to education, public policy can provide incentives for behavioral change. Governments can introduce plastic tax policies or deposit return schemes, which encourage consumers to return used plastic products for recycling by offering a financial incentive. These policies not only promote recycling but also raise awareness about the need to reduce plastic waste and recycle more effectively.

The Role of Technology in Supporting Behavioral Change

While behavioral change is often seen through the lens of individual actions and education, technology can also play a vital role in supporting these efforts. Advances in mobile apps and digital platforms have allowed consumers to easily track their plastic usage, access recycling information, and participate in sustainability challenges. For example, some apps enable users to scan product packaging and check if it is recyclable or if it contains sustainable materials, helping individuals make informed purchasing decisions. Other apps allow people to track their progress in reducing plastic consumption, providing motivation and accountability.

Technological innovations also support smart waste management systems, which use sensors and data analytics to optimize waste collection and recycling processes. These systems can help increase recycling rates by making it easier for consumers to properly dispose of plastic waste, ensuring that materials are sorted correctly and reducing contamination.

Alternative Materials and Innovations

As the world grapples with the escalating plastic waste crisis, finding effective alternatives to traditional plastic materials has become a key focus in the push for sustainability. Bamboo, glass, edible packaging, and other innovative materials have emerged as potential substitutes for plastic in a variety of applications. These alternatives not only offer environmentally friendly solutions but also present unique challenges in terms of scalability, cost, and performance. This section explores these alternative materials, evaluating their feasibility in replacing plastic in various sectors, and examines the innovations that are driving this transition toward more sustainable materials.

Exploring Alternatives Like Bamboo, Glass, and Edible Packaging

Bamboo has emerged as a popular alternative to plastic, particularly in the packaging, textiles, and consumer goods sectors. Bamboo is a fast-growing, renewable resource that requires little water, making it an environmentally friendly choice. Its fibers are strong and durable, and bamboo can be used to create a variety of products that are typically made from plastic, such as straws, cutlery, toothbrushes, and even clothing. Bamboo's natural properties make it biodegradable, which is a major advantage over plastic, as it decomposes relatively quickly without leaving harmful residues.

The use of bamboo for packaging is one of its most promising applications. Companies are increasingly turning to bamboo-based packaging materials to replace single-use plastic packaging for food products, electronics, and other consumer goods. For instance, bamboo pulp is being used to create eco-friendly packaging that is lightweight, durable, and biodegradable. These packaging solutions offer significant reductions in plastic waste, particularly in industries such as food packaging, where bamboo-based containers are becoming more common. However, there are challenges to consider, such as the cost and infrastructure required for large-scale bamboo cultivation and processing. Additionally, the production of bamboo products, though generally less resource-intensive than plastics, still requires energy and materials, so the full environmental impact must be considered.

Glass is another alternative that is gaining traction as a replacement for plastic, especially in the beverage and food packaging sectors. Glass containers, such as bottles and jars, have been used for centuries and are favored for their ability to preserve the freshness and quality of food and drinks. Glass is fully recyclable and can be reused indefinitely without losing quality, making it a highly sustainable material. Unlike plastic, glass does not leach harmful chemicals into food or drinks, making it a preferred choice for health-conscious consumers.

The main drawback of glass as an alternative to plastic is its weight, which makes it more costly to transport. The heavy nature of glass also contributes to higher carbon emissions during transportation, particularly when shipping large volumes of goods. Additionally, glass production is energy-intensive, requiring high temperatures to melt and mold the material, which can contribute to its environmental impact. However, the recyclability of glass and its long-lasting properties make it a strong candidate for replacing plastic in certain markets, particularly where packaging durability and safety are critical, such as in the food and beverage industry.

Edible packaging is one of the most innovative alternatives to traditional plastic packaging. Made from natural, biodegradable ingredients such as seaweed, rice, or gelatin, edible packaging is designed to be consumed along with the product it contains, eliminating the need for disposal. This type of packaging has gained attention in the food industry, where it is used to package snacks, condiments, and beverages. One notable example is seaweed-based packaging, which can be molded into various shapes and sizes and used to package liquids or solid food items. Seaweed is a sustainable and renewable resource that grows rapidly and does not require large amounts of water or land to cultivate.

The advantages of edible packaging are clear: it reduces plastic waste and provides an innovative, functional solution to food packaging. However, there are challenges to overcome in terms of scalability, cost, and consumer acceptance. Producing edible packaging in large quantities may be more expensive than conventional plastic packaging, and some consumers may be hesitant to embrace the idea of eating packaging. Additionally, edible packaging must meet strict food safety and hygiene standards, which adds to its complexity and cost. Despite these challenges, edible packaging represents a fascinating and eco-friendly alternative that could revolutionize the way we think about packaging waste in the future.

The Feasibility of Replacing Plastic in Various Sectors

While alternatives such as bamboo, glass, and edible packaging offer exciting possibilities, the feasibility of replacing plastic across various sectors is not without its challenges. The transition from plastic to sustainable materials requires careful consideration of factors such as cost, performance, consumer behavior, and industry-specific needs.

In the food and beverage industry, the demand for plastic packaging is vast, as plastic is lightweight, durable, and inexpensive. Glass and bamboo-based packaging have the potential to replace plastic in some food packaging applications, but their higher production costs and the need for specialized infrastructure may limit their widespread adoption. For example, glass bottles are ideal for beverages like juices and soft drinks, but their weight and higher transportation costs can make them less attractive for products sold in bulk or in regions with limited access to glass recycling systems. Similarly, bamboo-based packaging may be suitable for certain food items but may not offer the same level of moisture resistance or barrier properties as plastic packaging.

In the retail and consumer goods sectors, the demand for single-use plastic packaging, such as bags, wraps, and containers, remains high due to its convenience and cost-effectiveness. Bamboo and other biodegradable materials can replace plastic in some applications, such as retail packaging and shopping bags, but scaling up the production of these alternatives to meet global demand may require significant investment. Additionally, recyclability remains a key concern; unlike plastics, which can often be recycled into new products, bamboo and other biodegradable materials typically degrade once they are composted and cannot be reused. For many consumer goods applications, these alternative materials may not yet offer the same functionality, shelf-life, or cost-effectiveness as plastic.

The electronics and automotive industries, which heavily rely on plastic for its versatility and performance, may face greater challenges in replacing plastic with alternative materials. Plastics play a crucial role in product design, offering lightweight, durable, and flexible solutions for components such as casings, panels, and interior elements. In these sectors, bioplastics and composite materials may offer promising alternatives, but they are still in the early stages of development and adoption. Furthermore, the performance and cost-effectiveness of these materials must meet the stringent requirements of high-tech industries, where durability and safety are paramount.

The medical industry also faces challenges in replacing plastic, particularly for single-use medical devices such as syringes, gloves, and packaging. While alternatives like glass and biodegradable materials can replace some plastic items, the sterilization and safety requirements in the medical sector make plastic the preferred material for many applications. Innovative solutions such as biodegradable polymers and compostable plastics may eventually offer viable alternatives, but their ability to meet medical standards for sterility, performance, and cost remains to be seen.

Corporate Responsibility and Collaboration

As the global plastic waste crisis deepens, the role of businesses in contributing to sustainable practices becomes more critical. Companies across industries must take responsibility for their environmental impact, particularly in the use of plastic materials, which account for a significant portion of global waste. Corporate responsibility encompasses a wide range of actions, from reducing plastic consumption and embracing alternative materials to improving recycling efforts and ensuring the responsible disposal of plastic products. Alongside individual company efforts, collaboration between government, industry, and civil society is essential for driving systemic change and creating a circular economy where plastic waste is minimized, and resources are reused efficiently. This section explores how businesses can shift toward more sustainable practices and the importance of collaboration in achieving lasting environmental change.

How Businesses Can Shift Toward Sustainable Practices

Businesses play a central role in addressing plastic waste, not only due to their contribution to plastic production and consumption but also because they possess the influence, resources, and scale necessary to drive change. Transitioning to more sustainable practices requires businesses to adopt comprehensive strategies that minimize plastic waste, improve resource efficiency, and ensure that their operations are aligned with broader environmental goals.

Reducing Plastic Consumption

The first step toward sustainability for many businesses is reducing their reliance on plastic. This can involve rethinking product design to eliminate unnecessary plastic packaging or replacing plastic materials with sustainable alternatives. For instance, businesses can explore options such as biodegradable plastics, plant-based plastics, glass, metal, or paper packaging. Retailers can encourage customers to bring their own reusable bags or containers, while food and beverage companies can transition to eco-friendly packaging that is either recyclable or compostable. Companies that produce products with a significant amount of plastic can also adopt minimalist packaging approaches, which reduce the overall plastic content while maintaining product integrity and convenience.

Embracing Circular Economy Principles

One of the most impactful shifts businesses can make is adopting circular economy principles, which aim to reduce waste and extend the lifecycle of products and materials. Companies can design products and packaging with recycling and reuse in mind, making them easier to recycle or repurpose at the end of their lifecycle. This could include implementing closed-loop systems, where materials are recycled back into the production process to create new products. By investing in sustainable materials and promoting the repair, reuse, and refurbishment of products, businesses can move away from the traditional "take, make, dispose" model and reduce the amount of plastic waste that ends up in landfills.

Improving Recycling Efforts

Businesses can also contribute significantly to the reduction of plastic waste by improving recycling efforts. Companies can collaborate with recycling facilities to ensure that their packaging is recyclable and that their products are designed to be easily disassembled and sorted. Additionally, they can invest in take-back programs or product stewardship initiatives, which allow consumers to return used products for recycling or responsible disposal. This is particularly important in industries such as electronics, where plastic components may contain valuable materials that can be reused in new products. Businesses can also educate consumers on how to properly recycle their products by providing clear instructions on packaging and investing in recycling infrastructure to ensure that materials are collected, sorted, and processed efficiently.

Setting Sustainability Goals and Tracking Progress

Corporate responsibility requires a strong commitment to sustainability and transparent accountability. Many businesses are now setting sustainability goals related to plastic use, waste reduction, and carbon emissions. By committing to specific, measurable targets—such as reducing plastic usage by a certain percentage or achieving zero plastic waste by a set date—companies can take concrete steps to track progress and hold themselves accountable. Several corporations have already set ambitious targets to reduce plastic packaging, with companies like Unilever, Coca-Cola, and Nestlé committing to make their packaging 100% recyclable, reusable, or compostable in the coming years. By publicly setting and reporting on such goals, businesses can demonstrate leadership in sustainability and encourage other companies to follow suit.

Adopting Green Innovation and Technology

Businesses should also consider investing in green innovations and new technologies that contribute to sustainable practices. For example, the development of chemical recycling technologies, which break down plastics into their original monomers for reuse, can increase the amount of plastic that is recycled and reduce the need for virgin plastic production. Businesses in the plastic production sector can work toward creating bio-based plastics or developing plastics that are easier to recycle and require fewer resources to produce. Investing in energy-efficient production processes and renewable energy sources is also essential for reducing the environmental footprint of manufacturing operations.

Collaboration Between Government, Industry, and Civil Society for Lasting Change

While individual businesses can make significant strides toward sustainability, systemic change requires collaboration between governments, industries, and civil society. No single sector can address the plastic waste crisis on its own. Governments, industries, and environmental organizations must work together to create policies, regulations, and initiatives that drive sustainable practices and promote innovation.

Government Role in Supporting Sustainability

Governments play a pivotal role in creating the regulatory framework necessary to reduce plastic waste and incentivize sustainable business practices. They can introduce and enforce EPR laws, which require businesses to take responsibility for the collection, recycling, and disposal of their products after they are sold. These laws shift the financial burden of waste management from taxpayers to producers, encouraging businesses to design products and packaging that are easier to recycle and less harmful to the environment.

Governments can also introduce plastic bans or plastic tax policies to discourage the use of single-use plastics. Many countries, including Kenya, France, and Bangladesh, have implemented strict bans on plastic bags, while others are exploring similar policies for other plastic products. Additionally, governments can provide incentives for businesses to adopt sustainable practices, such as offering subsidies for companies that use recycled materials or that invest in green technologies.

Industry Collaboration for Innovation and Scale

To drive innovation and ensure the large-scale adoption of sustainable practices, industries must collaborate across supply chains and sectors. Business alliances, such as the Ellen MacArthur Foundation's New Plastics Economy initiative, have brought together global corporations, NGOs, and governments to create a circular economy for plastics. These collaborations enable businesses to share knowledge, resources, and technologies, helping to accelerate the transition to more sustainable business practices. Collaborative efforts can include investing in joint recycling programs, sharing best practices in product design, and pooling resources to develop alternative materials and technologies.

Collaboration between industries is also crucial in addressing the global nature of plastic waste. As plastics are often produced in one region and consumed in another, international partnerships are necessary to create global solutions for plastic waste management. Transnational agreements, such as the Basel Convention on the control of hazardous waste, can help standardize recycling systems, improve waste management practices, and reduce plastic pollution.

Engaging Civil Society and Consumers

Civil society organizations, such as environmental groups, grassroots movements, and advocacy organizations, are essential in pushing for policy change and holding businesses accountable. These organizations raise awareness about the impact of plastic pollution, advocate for more sustainable policies, and educate consumers about reducing plastic waste. Collaboration between businesses and civil society organizations can help ensure that sustainability initiatives align with public concerns and lead to tangible results.

Consumer behavior is another critical factor in driving business change. Consumer demand for sustainable products and packaging has prompted many companies to invest in eco-friendly alternatives. By prioritizing sustainability in purchasing decisions, consumers have the power to influence business practices and encourage companies to adopt greener solutions. Civil society organizations can play a key role in mobilizing consumers through awareness campaigns, petitions, and consumer advocacy.

Technological Innovation and Breakthroughs

The push to reduce plastic waste has catalyzed a wave of technological innovations aimed at developing biodegradable materials and eco-friendly plastics. These innovations are critical to addressing the plastic pollution crisis, as traditional plastic products take hundreds of years to break down and often end up in landfills or the natural environment. Innovations such as biodegradable plastics, algae-based plastics, and fungi packaging offer promising alternatives to petroleum-based plastics, reducing environmental impact and contributing to a more sustainable future. This section explores the advancements in these technologies, their potential applications, and the challenges associated with scaling them up for widespread use.

Innovations in Biodegradable Materials and Eco-Friendly Plastics

Biodegradable plastics are designed to break down more easily in the environment, reducing their persistence in ecosystems. These materials are typically derived from renewable sources, such as corn starch, sugarcane, and potato starch, which can be processed into plastic-like substances. Unlike conventional plastics, which can take centuries to decompose, biodegradable plastics degrade over a much shorter time, depending on environmental conditions. The two primary types of biodegradable plastics are PHA and PLA, both of which have gained significant attention for their potential to replace traditional plastic packaging.

• PHA are biodegradable plastics produced by microorganisms through the fermentation of organic materials such as sugars, vegetable oils, or plant starches. PHAs are highly versatile and can be used in a variety of applications, including packaging, agricultural films, and medical products. The biodegradability of PHAs in both aerobic and anaerobic conditions makes them an attractive alternative to petroleum-based plastics, especially for use in marine environments, where plastic waste is a growing concern. However, the production of PHAs can be expensive due to the cost of raw materials and the energy-intensive fermentation process. Scaling up production and reducing costs remain significant challenges.

• PLA is another type of biodegradable plastic made from renewable resources such as corn starch or sugarcane. PLA is one of the most widely used biodegradable plastics and is commonly found in food packaging, disposable cutlery, and plastic bottles. PLA can be composted in industrial composting facilities, where it breaks down into natural elements. While PLA is biodegradable, it does not degrade in natural environments like soil or water as quickly as PHAs. It also requires specific conditions, such as high temperatures, to decompose efficiently. Nevertheless, PLA has been embraced by many companies looking to reduce their reliance on petroleum-based plastics, especially in the food and beverage industry.

• Eco-friendly plastics, also known as bioplastics, include not only biodegradable plastics like PHA and PLA but also plastics made from plant-based materials such as bio-based polyethylene (Bio-PE) or bio-based polypropylene (Bio-PP). These plastics are produced from renewable resources, such as sugarcane, corn, or algae, and offer a more sustainable alternative to traditional plastics made from fossil fuels. Bio-based plastics have the same chemical structure and properties as their petroleum-based counterparts but are produced with a lower carbon footprint. However, while bio-based plastics are a step forward in terms of sustainability, they still face challenges related to recycling, compostability, and the environmental impact of their production processes.

Despite their potential, biodegradable and eco-friendly plastics face several challenges that hinder their widespread adoption. The production costs of these materials are generally higher than traditional plastics, particularly for PHAs. Additionally, the infrastructure required for industrial composting is not yet widely available in many regions, which limits the effectiveness of PLA and other biodegradable plastics. Furthermore, these materials may not always be as durable or versatile as traditional plastics, which can affect their functionality in certain applications. Continued innovation and investment in production processes, recycling technologies, and infrastructure are needed to make biodegradable plastics a mainstream solution to plastic waste.

Advances in Plastic Alternatives: Algae-Based Plastics and Fungi Packaging

In recent years, algae-based plastics and fungi packaging have emerged as exciting and innovative alternatives to conventional plastics. These materials are made from natural, renewable resources and offer promising solutions to the plastic waste crisis, thanks to their biodegradability and low environmental impact.

Algae-Based Plastics

Algae-based plastics are made from algae biomass, which is harvested from various types of algae, including seaweed and microalgae. Algae-based plastics are considered highly sustainable due to the fast growth rate of algae and its ability to capture carbon dioxide during photosynthesis. Unlike traditional plastic production, which relies on petrochemicals, algae-based plastics offer a renewable source of material that does not compete with food production, making it a more sustainable alternative.

The process of creating algae-based plastics involves extracting the polymers and carbohydrates from algae and processing them into a plastic-like material. These plastics can be molded into various forms, such as packaging, bags, and containers, and have similar properties to conventional plastics, including flexibility, durability, and resistance to moisture. Moreover, algae-based plastics are biodegradable, meaning they can break down in natural environments like soil or water without causing long-term pollution.

Algae-based plastics have several advantages over traditional plastics. First, they are carbon-negative, as algae absorb carbon dioxide while growing. Second, algae are highly efficient at converting sunlight into energy, making them an environmentally friendly resource. Third, algae-based plastics are biodegradable and can decompose relatively quickly when exposed to natural elements, unlike conventional plastics that can persist in the environment for hundreds of years. However, challenges remain in scaling up the production of algae-based plastics. Algae farming is still in the early stages of development, and large-scale cultivation of algae for plastic production requires significant investment in infrastructure, research, and technology.

Fungi Packaging

Fungi packaging is another innovative alternative to plastic that has gained attention in recent years. This material is made from mycelium, the root structure of fungi, which is combined with organic waste, such as agricultural by-products, to create a lightweight, biodegradable material. The process of producing fungi-based packaging involves growing mycelium in molds, where it forms a dense, durable material that can be used for packaging products.

Fungi packaging is biodegradable and can break down naturally in the environment without causing pollution. It also offers the advantage of being made from waste materials, making it a highly sustainable option for packaging. Moreover, the production process for fungi packaging is energy-efficient and can be done with minimal resources. Mycelium grows rapidly, and the material can be produced using low-tech methods, making it an ideal solution for areas with limited industrial infrastructure.

Fungi packaging has a wide range of applications, from protective packaging for electronics and fragile items to food packaging and insulation materials. The material is strong, lightweight, and highly customizable, allowing it to be shaped into various forms to suit different products. It is also non-toxic and safe for food contact, making it a viable alternative to plastic in the food packaging industry. However, scaling up the production of fungi packaging and reducing the cost of materials are significant challenges. As with algae-based plastics, fungi packaging is still in the early stages of commercialization, and further investment in research, development, and infrastructure is needed to make it a viable alternative to plastic packaging on a large scale.

The Future of Plastic Alternatives

The innovations in biodegradable materials, algae-based plastics, and fungi packaging represent significant breakthroughs in the quest to reduce plastic waste and transition to more sustainable materials. These technologies are promising, as they offer biodegradable, renewable alternatives to traditional plastics that can help reduce plastic pollution and its harmful environmental impacts. However, there are still challenges to overcome in terms of scalability, cost, and performance.

For these alternative materials to replace plastic on a large scale, continued research and development will be essential to improve their performance, reduce production costs, and increase their commercial viability. As industries and governments invest in sustainable materials and infrastructure, and as consumer demand for eco-friendly products continues to rise, these alternative materials may play a crucial role in reducing the global reliance on plastic and fostering a more sustainable, circular economy.

Policy and Legal Solutions

As the global plastic waste crisis continues to escalate, policy and legal frameworks are essential in creating a structured approach to curbing plastic production, reducing consumption, and improving recycling efforts. Governments and international bodies must strengthen international agreements and enforce local laws to effectively tackle the environmental challenges posed by plastic pollution. This section explores how strengthening these frameworks can help curb plastic production and consumption, as well as how incentives can be created to encourage businesses, consumers, and industries to adopt more sustainable practices. Ultimately, robust policy and legal solutions are crucial to achieving a future free of plastic waste.

Strengthening International Agreements and Local Laws to Curb Plastic Production

International cooperation is vital in addressing the global plastic waste issue, as plastic pollution is a transnational problem. Plastics that are discarded in one country often end up in the oceans or ecosystems of another, affecting biodiversity, wildlife, and human communities around the world. Strengthening international agreements and frameworks to curb plastic production can ensure that nations work together to reduce plastic waste at a global scale.

One of the most significant international agreements related to plastic waste is the Basel Convention, which was amended in 2019 to include plastic waste in its scope. The Basel Convention, a treaty originally created to regulate the transboundary movement of hazardous waste, now covers the movement of plastic waste between countries. The amendment aims to prevent plastic waste from being illegally exported to developing countries that lack the infrastructure to manage it effectively. By regulating the export and import of plastic waste, the Basel Convention seeks to reduce the accumulation of plastic in regions where it can cause severe environmental damage.

Another important international framework is the UNEP, which has been instrumental in raising global awareness about the plastic waste crisis. UNEP launched the Clean Seas Campaign in 2017, which encourages governments and businesses to take action to reduce plastic pollution. This campaign promotes the adoption of policies such as plastic bag bans, EPR, and stricter regulations on the production and disposal of plastic. Through UNEP, countries can collaborate on best practices, share knowledge, and align their policies to tackle plastic pollution more effectively.

However, while these international agreements are a step in the right direction, there is still a need for stronger, more binding commitments to curb plastic production globally. Plastic production is increasing, driven by the demand for cheap, versatile materials used in packaging, consumer products, and electronics. Many countries continue to subsidize plastic production, which makes it more economically attractive than sustainable alternatives. International agreements should focus on establishing concrete limits on plastic production, encouraging the use of alternative materials, and fostering global recycling infrastructure to ensure that plastics are reused rather than discarded.

On the national level, local laws play a crucial role in regulating plastic use and waste management. Countries such as Kenya, France, and India have implemented stringent plastic bans to curb plastic pollution, specifically targeting single-use plastics such as bags, straws, and packaging. These laws have had a significant impact on reducing plastic waste and encouraging the use of alternatives.

However, enforcement of such laws can be challenging, especially in developing countries or regions where informal waste management systems are prevalent.

One effective legal tool for addressing plastic waste is the implementation of EPR laws. EPR laws place the responsibility for the collection, recycling, and disposal of plastic products on manufacturers and producers, rather than consumers or governments. Under such laws, businesses are required to take back their products at the end of their lifecycle and ensure they are properly recycled or disposed of. This approach encourages manufacturers to design products with sustainability in mind, reducing the use of non-recyclable materials and promoting the use of more eco-friendly packaging. Several European countries, including Germany and the Netherlands, have successfully implemented EPR schemes for plastic packaging, and other nations should consider adopting similar policies to reduce plastic waste.

Creating Incentives for the Reduction of Plastic Use and Boosting Recycling Efforts

Incentives are a powerful tool in driving behavioral change at the individual, business, and government levels. By creating financial, social, and regulatory incentives, policymakers can encourage the adoption of sustainable practices, such as reducing plastic consumption, improving recycling efforts, and transitioning to more sustainable materials.

Financial Incentives for Businesses

Governments can create incentives for businesses to adopt sustainable practices by offering subsidies, tax credits, and grants for companies that reduce their plastic usage, invest in alternative materials, or improve their recycling infrastructure. These financial incentives can offset the initial costs of transitioning to more sustainable packaging and production methods, making it easier for businesses to adopt eco-friendly practices. For example, businesses that use biodegradable materials or plant-based plastics instead of petroleum-based plastics could be eligible for tax reductions or grants to support the development and scaling of these alternatives. Similarly, governments could incentivize businesses to invest in closed-loop recycling systems, which ensure that plastic materials are continuously reused and repurposed rather than discarded.

DRS

One of the most effective ways to encourage recycling is through DRS, which incentivize consumers to return their used plastic bottles and containers for recycling. In these systems, consumers pay a small deposit when purchasing a product and receive a refund when the empty container is returned to a collection point. DRS has been proven to significantly increase recycling rates by making it easier for consumers to recycle and providing a financial incentive to return plastic products. Countries like Germany, Norway, and Finland have successfully implemented DRS, and many other countries are exploring the adoption of similar systems. Expanding these programs to include more types of plastic products and making them more widely accessible could play a crucial role in increasing global plastic recycling rates.

Plastic Taxation and Regulation

Another policy solution is the implementation of plastic taxation, which imposes fees on the production and use of plastic materials, particularly single-use plastics. This tax serves as a financial deterrent to the overproduction and consumption of plastics, encouraging businesses to reduce plastic packaging and consumers to opt for more sustainable alternatives. For example, the plastic bag tax implemented in the United Kingdom in 2015 led to a dramatic reduction in the use of single-use plastic bags, with a significant decrease in plastic waste associated with bags. By applying similar taxes to other single-use plastics, governments can create a market shift toward alternatives like reusable bags, containers, and packaging. Additionally, plastic production taxes could be used to fund recycling programs or promote research and development into more sustainable plastic alternatives.

Encouraging Corporate Responsibility

Governments can also create incentives for businesses to adopt more sustainable practices by encouraging corporate responsibility. Companies that publicly commit to reducing plastic waste, transitioning to eco-friendly materials, and adopting circular economy models can be recognized through certifications, eco-labels, or public recognition. For example, the B Corp certification, which is awarded to companies that meet high social and environmental standards, could be expanded to include plastic waste reduction as a key criterion. Governments could also introduce green procurement policies, where public contracts are awarded to companies that demonstrate sustainable practices, including reduced plastic use.

Public Education Campaigns

In addition to legal and financial incentives, public education campaigns are essential to raise awareness about the environmental impact of plastic waste and encourage consumers to reduce their plastic consumption. Governments and environmental organizations can use media, social platforms, and educational programs to inform the public about the importance of reducing plastic waste, recycling properly, and supporting companies that prioritize sustainability. These campaigns can help change consumer behaviors, creating a cultural shift toward sustainable consumption patterns.

Strengthening international agreements and local laws, combined with the creation of incentives for reducing plastic use and improving recycling efforts, is essential to tackling the global plastic waste crisis. By reinforcing international frameworks like the Basel Convention and UNEP's Clean Seas Campaign, governments can create a unified approach to curb plastic production and waste. On the local level, policies such as plastic bans, extended producer responsibility laws, and deposit return schemes can provide the necessary legal and financial frameworks to reduce plastic waste and increase recycling rates.

Chapter 6: Case Studies in Plastic Waste Management

Chapter 6 presents a collection of case studies that highlight successful initiatives and strategies for plastic waste management across the globe. By examining real-world examples from diverse regions and sectors, this chapter aims to demonstrate the effectiveness of various approaches to tackling plastic pollution. These case studies cover a range of topics, from innovative waste management systems and corporate responsibility initiatives to community-driven recycling programs. Through these examples, the chapter provides valuable insights into the challenges, successes, and lessons learned from different efforts to manage plastic waste, offering practical solutions that can be adapted and scaled to address the growing global plastic pollution crisis.

Successful Global Models

As plastic waste continues to be a global environmental challenge, several countries and cities have emerged as leaders in reducing plastic consumption, improving waste management systems, and promoting sustainability. By implementing innovative policies, encouraging community involvement, and investing in infrastructure, these nations and cities have made significant strides in tackling plastic waste and setting an example for others to follow. This section examines some of the most successful global models for plastic waste reduction, highlighting the policies and initiatives that have demonstrated tangible impacts.

Countries and Cities Leading the Way in Reducing Plastic Waste

Several countries and cities around the world have adopted aggressive policies to reduce plastic waste and promote sustainability. These efforts vary in scope, from nationwide plastic bans to city-specific recycling initiatives. What they share in common is a commitment to addressing the environmental threat posed by plastic pollution and a determination to lead by example.

Kenya: A Bold Plastic Bag Ban

In 2017, Kenya became one of the first countries in the world to impose a nationwide ban on plastic bags, one of the most widely used forms of plastic waste. The ban was implemented as part of Kenya's broader efforts to combat plastic pollution, particularly in urban areas and in the country's extensive agricultural sector. Kenya's plastic bag ban has been hailed as one of the strictest in the world, with severe penalties for offenders, including hefty fines and jail time for manufacturers, distributors, and retailers who violate the ban.

The policy has had a significant impact on reducing plastic waste in Kenya. Plastic bags, once ubiquitous in both urban and rural areas, have largely disappeared from the environment. The initiative has also spurred innovation in alternatives to plastic bags, with many businesses and consumers turning to reusable bags made from cloth, jute, or other eco-friendly materials. However, the success of this policy has not come without challenges. Enforcement in remote areas and among informal markets remains difficult, and there are concerns about the limited availability of alternative products. Nevertheless, Kenya's bold stance on plastic bags has positioned it as a global leader in addressing plastic pollution.

Germany: Pioneering Waste Management and Recycling

Germany is a global model for efficient waste management and recycling. The country's dual system of recycling, established in the early 1990s, has become a blueprint for many other nations seeking to improve their waste management systems. The Green Dot system, a nationwide recycling program, requires companies to take responsibility for the waste generated by their products. Businesses must pay for the collection, recycling, or disposal of packaging waste, which incentivizes them to reduce the use of non-recyclable materials and adopt more sustainable packaging solutions.

Germany has one of the highest recycling rates in the world, with approximately 67% of its waste being recycled. The country's waste management system is characterized by well-developed infrastructure for sorting and processing waste, including dedicated recycling bins for different materials and a strong emphasis on separating plastics from other waste. Germany's EPR laws have played a crucial role in encouraging companies to minimize plastic packaging, and its nationwide deposit return system (DRS) for beverage containers has significantly boosted recycling rates. The success of Germany's waste management model can be attributed to comprehensive policies, consumer participation, and robust infrastructure that supports recycling at all levels.

France: Tackling Single-Use Plastics

In 2020, France implemented a sweeping ban on single-use plastics as part of its commitment to environmental sustainability. The Plastic Waste Reduction Act, which came into effect in January 2020, includes measures to phase out single-use plastic items, such as plastic straws, plates, and cutlery, as well as plastic packaging for fruits and vegetables. The law also mandates that businesses transition to compostable or biodegradable alternatives for plastic items, with a focus on sustainable packaging.

France's efforts to reduce plastic waste are part of its broader commitment to achieving zero plastic waste by 2040. The country has made significant progress in reducing the consumption of single-use plastics, with several businesses adopting sustainable practices in packaging and production. The ban on plastic plates and cutlery has encouraged the use of biodegradable alternatives made from materials such as cornstarch, sugarcane, and bamboo. In addition, France has introduced initiatives to promote recycling and encourage circular economy practices, such as improving waste sorting and investing in recycling technologies.

While France's efforts have been met with some resistance from industries reliant on plastic products, the Plastic Waste Reduction Act represents a bold step forward in addressing the plastic pollution crisis. France's ambitious goals and strong regulatory framework are expected to set an example for other European countries and inspire further action in the fight against plastic waste.

South Korea: Advanced Recycling and Waste-to-Energy Systems

South Korea has emerged as a leader in WtE technologies and advanced recycling systems. The country boasts one of the highest recycling rates in the world, with an impressive rate of 53% of household waste being recycled. South Korea's waste management system is characterized by its efficient sorting and collection infrastructure, which ensures that recyclable materials, including plastics, are separated from general waste.

In addition to its recycling systems, South Korea has invested heavily in waste-to-energy technologies, which convert waste materials into electricity and heat. The country has implemented an extensive network of incinerators that recover energy from non-recyclable plastic waste, helping to reduce landfill use and generate renewable energy. However, the environmental impact of incineration remains a topic of debate, as it releases carbon emissions, which may offset some of the environmental benefits.

South Korea has also introduced PAYT policies, which charge residents based on the amount of waste they generate. This incentivizes consumers to reduce waste and recycle more effectively. The combination of advanced recycling, waste-to-energy systems, and economic incentives has helped South Korea significantly reduce its plastic waste and improve its waste management systems.

Analysis of Policies and Initiatives That Have Shown Significant Impact

The success of these countries and cities in reducing plastic waste can be attributed to several key factors, including strong government leadership, effective policy implementation, innovative waste management systems, and public engagement.

Comprehensive Policies and Legal Frameworks

One of the most important factors contributing to successful plastic waste management models is the implementation of comprehensive, well-enforced policies. Countries like Kenya and France have demonstrated that plastic bans can significantly reduce plastic consumption when paired with clear regulations, enforcement mechanisms, and alternative solutions. EPR laws, such as those seen in Germany, are also effective in shifting the responsibility for plastic waste onto manufacturers, encouraging them to design products with recyclability in mind and to take responsibility for the waste generated.

Public Participation and Awareness

The success of these policies relies heavily on public participation and awareness. Germany's high recycling rate is largely attributed to its extensive public education programs and the widespread acceptance of recycling practices. South Korea's pay-as-you-throw system, which incentivizes waste reduction, has also been successful because it encourages consumers to actively engage in the recycling process. Public participation is essential in ensuring the success of policies and initiatives, and governments must invest in education campaigns to raise awareness about the importance of reducing plastic waste and recycling properly.

Innovative Waste Management Systems

Cities and countries that have invested in advanced waste sorting technologies, recycling infrastructure, and waste-to-energy systems have seen significant reductions in plastic waste. South Korea's waste-to-energy initiatives are a prime example of how innovation can be used to address plastic waste while generating renewable energy. Germany's dual system of recycling and Green Dot system provide effective models for other countries seeking to improve their recycling infrastructure. These systems ensure that recyclable materials, including plastics, are efficiently sorted, processed, and reused, reducing the amount of waste sent to landfills.

Community-Level Solutions

As global plastic waste continues to pose significant environmental and health risks, community-level solutions are emerging as crucial players in the broader efforts to reduce plastic pollution. Grassroots movements and community-led plastic waste reduction efforts have demonstrated the power of local action in tackling plastic waste. These initiatives often take root in neighborhoods, small towns, or informal sectors, where residents and local organizations work together to address the issue at the grassroots level. The success of these initiatives lies in their ability to foster community involvement, increase local awareness, and create sustainable, context-specific solutions. This section explores the role of grassroots movements and small-scale initiatives in reducing plastic waste, focusing on examples from developing countries and highlighting the impact of community-driven efforts.

Grassroots Movements and Community-Led Plastic Waste Reduction Efforts

Grassroots movements are bottom-up efforts that often emerge organically from communities that are directly affected by plastic pollution. These movements rely on the collective action of individuals, local organizations, and community groups to address the pressing issue of plastic waste. They are typically more nimble and adaptable than large-scale government initiatives, as they are directly in tune with the unique needs and circumstances of the communities they serve.

One of the defining features of grassroots movements is their ability to mobilize local resources and engage community members in practical actions. These movements often involve education campaigns, clean-up efforts, and the promotion of alternatives to plastic, such as reusable bags or compostable packaging. In many cases, these movements are born from a sense of urgency and frustration, as communities experience firsthand the detrimental impacts of plastic waste, such as blocked drainage systems, polluted waterways, and wildlife harm.

For example, the Plastic Free July campaign, which started as a grassroots movement in Australia, has now become a global phenomenon. The initiative encourages individuals to reduce their plastic consumption for one month by avoiding single-use plastics and finding alternative solutions. Over the years, the campaign has inspired communities around the world to come together, host events, and share solutions for reducing plastic waste. The power of this initiative lies in its simplicity and its ability to bring people together through a shared commitment to sustainability.

In many cases, grassroots movements evolve into more organized efforts, creating networks of community leaders, NGOs, and activists who continue to raise awareness and promote sustainable practices. These movements often act as catalysts for policy change, pressuring local governments and businesses to adopt more sustainable practices and adopt policies such as plastic bag bans or increased recycling efforts. Community-led clean-ups and plastic waste reduction workshops are common activities that empower local people to take control of the issue within their neighborhoods.

Examples from Developing Countries and Small-Scale Initiatives

Many of the most successful community-led plastic waste reduction efforts have emerged in developing countries, where access to formal waste management systems may be limited, and where plastic pollution can have particularly dire consequences for public health and the environment. In these regions, local communities are often left to fend for themselves in managing plastic waste, leading to the development of small-scale, innovative solutions that directly address local needs.

India: Plastic-Free Villages and Community Recycling Programs

In India, plastic pollution is a significant challenge, particularly in rural areas and urban slums, where waste management infrastructure is often underdeveloped or non-existent. However, several grassroots initiatives in India have shown the power of local action in addressing the issue of plastic waste. One such initiative is the Plastic-Free Village movement, which began in the state of Kerala. The movement aims to eliminate single-use plastic from villages by promoting alternatives and engaging local communities in waste management.

In Kerala, communities have organized plastic collection drives, recycling programs, and awareness campaigns to reduce plastic waste. These initiatives have been successful in getting local residents to not only eliminate plastic bags but also to recycle plastic items and participate in community clean-up activities. In some areas, villagers have established waste segregation systems and work with local recycling businesses to convert plastic waste into valuable products, such as building materials or sustainable packaging.

These community-led efforts have shown that small-scale initiatives can be highly effective in reducing plastic waste in regions where formal waste management services are lacking. The success of the Plastic-Free Village movement has inspired similar programs in other parts of India and has led to greater local involvement in plastic waste management.

Kenya: Community-Led Beach Clean-Ups and Plastic Collection

In Kenya, plastic waste has become a major concern, especially in coastal areas where plastic debris often washes up on beaches and pollutes the ocean. In response, several grassroots organizations have launched community-led beach clean-up campaigns and plastic waste management programs aimed at cleaning the coastline and reducing plastic waste in marine environments.

One of the most prominent organizations involved in plastic waste reduction on Kenya's coast is the CoastCare Kenya initiative, which brings together local communities, environmental groups, and schools to participate in regular beach clean-ups. These clean-up events not only help remove plastic waste from the beaches but also serve as educational opportunities for community members, teaching them about the dangers of plastic pollution and how to reduce their plastic consumption.

Through these clean-up campaigns, communities have been able to remove large amounts of plastic from their local environment, significantly improving the condition of beaches and reducing the harmful impact on marine life. Additionally, local businesses have been encouraged to adopt sustainable packaging and reduce the use of single-use plastics. The success of these efforts has resulted in policy advocacy for stronger anti-plastic regulations, including the plastic bag ban that Kenya implemented in 2017.

Philippines: Waste-to-Energy Initiatives and Eco-Friendly Alternatives

In the Philippines, where plastic waste is a growing problem, several community-based initiatives have emerged that focus on waste-to-energy technologies and the promotion of eco-friendly alternatives to plastic. One such initiative is the "Zero Waste" project in the city of Quezon. This initiative encourages residents to reduce, reuse, and recycle their waste by providing composting programs, recycling workshops, and opportunities for community members to exchange plastic waste for eco-friendly products.

The Quezon City program has proven successful in engaging local residents in waste reduction efforts, particularly in the informal settlements where access to formal waste management services is limited. Residents are encouraged to participate in community composting and recycling efforts, helping to reduce the amount of plastic waste that ends up in landfills or the environment. The initiative also educates the public on eco-friendly alternatives to plastic, such as biodegradable packaging and reusable containers.

Another successful initiative in the Philippines focuses on waste-to-energy technologies, where local communities convert plastic waste into biogas or electricity through anaerobic digestion or pyrolysis. These small-scale, community-led waste-to-energy projects provide an environmentally sustainable way to reduce plastic waste while generating renewable energy for local communities.

Small-Scale Initiatives and Local Solutions

In addition to the large-scale, community-led programs discussed above, many smaller, localized initiatives are also having a significant impact on reducing plastic waste. These initiatives often focus on product innovation, alternative materials, and local waste management solutions.

Small-Scale Recycling Centers

In several developing countries, small-scale recycling centers have been established in urban and rural communities. These centers often serve as hubs for collecting, sorting, and processing plastic waste that might otherwise end up in landfills or informal dumpsites. Community members work together to sort plastic waste into different categories, such as PET bottles, plastic bags, and polystyrene, and then send these materials to larger recycling facilities or repurpose them into new products.

Promoting Alternatives to Plastic

Small businesses and local artisans in developing countries are increasingly turning to eco-friendly alternatives to plastic, including materials such as bamboo, woven fibers, and leaf-based products. In rural areas of countries like India and Indonesia, traditional knowledge and local resources are being used to produce packaging materials that are biodegradable and less harmful to the environment. These alternatives not only reduce reliance on plastic but also promote local economic development by creating jobs and providing income opportunities.

Innovative Industry Solutions

The plastic waste crisis is one of the most significant environmental challenges of our time, and addressing it requires innovative solutions across multiple sectors. Corporations and startups are at the forefront of developing cutting-edge technologies and sustainable alternatives to plastic. Through creative product design, new materials, and alternative production processes, businesses are taking responsibility for reducing plastic waste. In addition, public-private partnerships are playing an increasingly critical role in driving systemic change by combining the resources, expertise, and capabilities of both sectors to foster large-scale solutions. This section explores how businesses and startups are addressing plastic waste through innovation and examines the importance of collaboration between public and private sectors in accelerating change.

Corporations and Startups Addressing Plastic Waste Through Innovation

Many large corporations and startups are increasingly recognizing the need to innovate in order to reduce plastic consumption and waste. With rising consumer demand for sustainable products and regulatory pressure, companies are investing heavily in research and development to create alternatives to plastic, improve recycling processes, and minimize plastic footprints across their supply chains.

Biodegradable Plastics and Sustainable Materials

Leading corporations are exploring biodegradable plastics and bio-based materials as alternatives to traditional plastics made from petroleum. One notable example is the Coca-Cola Company, which is working to reduce the use of single-use plastic bottles by exploring alternatives such as plant-based plastics and biodegradable materials. Coca-Cola has committed to using 100% recyclable or compostable packaging by 2025, and it is experimenting with plant-based PET bottles (PET made from plants instead of petroleum) in partnership with Danone and Nestlé. Additionally, the company is working to make its packaging materials easier to recycle and exploring ways to reduce plastic packaging in favor of more sustainable options.

Another example of corporate innovation is Unilever, a global consumer goods company known for its commitment to sustainability. Unilever has made significant strides in reducing plastic waste through initiatives like using recycled plastic in its packaging and exploring compostable packaging options. The company has also committed to reducing plastic use by 50% by 2025 and aims to achieve a zero-waste target in its supply chain. Unilever's efforts to collaborate with other industry leaders, governments, and organizations in sustainability have made it a key player in promoting innovative solutions to plastic waste.

In the startup ecosystem, companies such as Loop and Bio-bean are pioneering new models of sustainability. Loop is a platform developed by TerraCycle, which allows consumers to buy products in reusable packaging, effectively eliminating single-use plastic containers. Through its partnerships with brands like Nestlé, Procter & Gamble, and Unilever, Loop is revolutionizing product packaging by offering products in durable, reusable containers that are returned, cleaned, and refilled.

Bio-bean, a UK-based startup, is taking a unique approach by turning coffee waste into a biodegradable plastic alternative. The company processes used coffee grounds into bio-plastics and biofuels, providing a sustainable alternative to petroleum-based plastics while helping reduce waste from the food and beverage industry. Bio-bean's innovative solution not only addresses plastic pollution but also provides a way to recycle waste into valuable, eco-friendly materials.

Recycling Innovations

One of the key challenges in plastic waste management is improving recycling rates and reducing contamination. To address this, corporations and startups are investing in advanced recycling technologies that can break down plastic more efficiently and process a wider range of materials. For example, Plastic Energy, a UK-based company, is pioneering chemical recycling processes that break down mixed plastics into their base components, which can then be used to create new plastic products. Unlike traditional mechanical recycling, which can only process clean, sorted plastics, chemical recycling enables the recycling of contaminated plastics, which are typically non-recyclable through conventional methods.

Another innovative startup, Gr3n, uses polymer depolymerization to recycle PET plastics into their raw monomers, making it possible to reuse them in new products without degrading their quality. This closed-loop recycling process could revolutionize the way we handle PET plastic waste, significantly reducing the need for virgin plastic production.

Additionally, some companies are experimenting with robotics and artificial intelligence (AI) to improve the efficiency of plastic sorting and recycling. AMP Robotics, for instance, uses AI-powered robots to automate the sorting of recyclables in waste facilities. These robots can identify and sort different types of plastics with greater speed and precision than manual sorting, improving the overall efficiency of recycling operations and reducing contamination.

Alternative Packaging Solutions

Many corporations are also focusing on alternative packaging solutions to reduce plastic waste. Companies like Aveda and Lush Cosmetics are already using biodegradable packaging made from sustainable materials like cornstarch or seaweed, which can decompose quickly and leave behind no harmful residues. Lush, for example, uses "naked" packaging for many of its products, such as shampoo bars and soap, which eliminate the need for plastic altogether.

In the food and beverage sector, Danone has developed plant-based plastic alternatives for yogurt containers. The company has created a line of products using biodegradable plastics made from natural materials like seaweed and coconut husks. These containers are biodegradable, reducing the environmental impact of the product's packaging and making it easier for consumers to dispose of waste responsibly.

Another notable initiative in the alternative packaging space comes from PepsiCo, which is exploring paper-based packaging and biodegradable plastics for its products. Through partnerships with Paptic and Danimer Scientific, PepsiCo aims to reduce the use of plastic packaging and introduce new alternatives that are both functional and sustainable.

Partnerships Between Public and Private Sectors to Drive Change

While individual companies and startups are taking important steps to innovate and reduce plastic waste, it is clear that a more holistic, systemic approach is needed to address the global scale of the problem. This is where public-private partnerships (PPPs) play a critical role in driving large-scale change. By combining the strengths of both sectors—governments' regulatory power and businesses' innovation and resources—PPPs can create sustainable solutions that benefit both the environment and the economy.

Collaborative Recycling Programs

In many countries, public-private partnerships are being leveraged to improve recycling infrastructure and increase the effectiveness of recycling programs. In Canada, the Packaging Consortium brings together businesses, environmental organizations, and government agencies to develop policies and programs that promote packaging sustainability. One of the consortium's initiatives is to encourage EPR for packaging, which holds manufacturers accountable for the waste their products generate.

In Germany, the Green Dot System is an example of a public-private partnership that has played a significant role in the country's high recycling rates. This system is run by Der Grüne Punkt, a non-profit organization that works with businesses and local governments to ensure that packaging is recyclable and that companies take responsibility for their waste. Through such partnerships, Germany has been able to achieve one of the highest recycling rates in the world, with nearly 70% of plastic packaging being recycled.

Innovation Hubs and Research Collaborations

Governments and private companies are also collaborating through innovation hubs and research initiatives to develop new materials, technologies, and processes for reducing plastic waste. One example is the New Plastics Economy initiative led by the Ellen MacArthur Foundation, which brings together businesses, governments, and academia to work on solutions that can reduce plastic waste and create a circular economy for plastics. This initiative has launched a series of research projects aimed at improving the recyclability of plastics, designing for a circular economy, and promoting alternatives to traditional plastic materials.

The Global Plastic Action Partnership (GPAP), a collaboration between the World Economic Forum and various public and private sector stakeholders, is working to identify sustainable solutions to plastic waste and develop global policies for waste management. Through partnerships with governments, industry leaders, and NGOs, GPAP is accelerating efforts to create a circular economy for plastics, aiming to reduce plastic pollution and encourage responsible plastic production and consumption.

Government Incentives and Corporate Collaboration

Governments are also creating incentives for businesses to invest in sustainability by providing financial support for eco-friendly innovations. Programs such as tax credits, subsidies, and research grants encourage businesses to explore alternatives to plastic packaging and invest in sustainable manufacturing processes. For example, the European Union's Circular Economy Action Plan provides financial incentives for companies that innovate in sustainable plastics and recycling. Through such policies, public-private collaborations are encouraging corporations to pursue circular economy models and develop sustainable solutions to reduce plastic waste.

Chapter 7: The Future of Plastic Waste

Chapter 7 explores the future of plastic waste, focusing on the emerging trends, technologies, and strategies that will shape how we address plastic pollution in the coming decades. As the world continues to grapple with the environmental impact of plastic, this chapter examines potential solutions, ranging from innovative recycling technologies to policy advancements and global collaborations. It looks at the challenges that lie ahead, such as scaling sustainable alternatives and achieving a circular economy, while also highlighting the opportunities for breakthrough innovations in plastic waste management. Ultimately, this chapter provides a forward-looking perspective on the role of technological advancements, regulatory frameworks, and collective global action in shaping a sustainable future free of plastic waste.

Predictions for Plastic Waste in the Coming Decades

As the world continues to grapple with the plastic waste crisis, understanding future trends in plastic production and waste generation is crucial for developing effective solutions. The use of plastic has increased dramatically over the past century, and with this growth comes the challenge of managing the resulting waste. Predictions for the coming decades suggest that unless urgent action is taken, plastic waste will continue to rise, leading to significant environmental, economic, and health impacts. This section explores the future trajectory of plastic production and waste trends, as well as the potential consequences of continuing current practices.

Estimating Future Plastic Production and Waste Trends

The global demand for plastic is expected to continue its upward trajectory in the coming decades. Plastics have become indispensable in numerous sectors, including packaging, construction, automotive, electronics, and healthcare, due to their versatility, lightweight properties, and cost-effectiveness. As populations grow, economies develop, and consumer demand for convenience continues to rise, the production of plastic is projected to increase accordingly. The global plastic production was estimated to be around 368 million metric tons in 2019, and projections indicate that this number could more than double by 2050 if current trends continue. Some estimates predict that plastic production will reach 1.1 billion metric tons by 2050, driven by demand from both developed and emerging economies.

Packaging is the largest single market for plastics, accounting for around 40% of global plastic consumption. As e-commerce continues to grow and consumer preferences for convenience-oriented products increase, the demand for plastic packaging—particularly single-use plastics—will likely remain strong. In fact, a 2021 report by the World Economic Forum (WEF) estimated that global plastic packaging will grow by 4% annually over the next decade. The food and beverage industry is a significant contributor to this growth, with plastic bottles, wrappers, straws, and single-serve containers being used extensively.

The automotive and electronics industries also contribute to the rising demand for plastic. Plastics are widely used in car parts, including dashboards, bumpers, and seats, and in electronic devices such as smartphones, computers, and appliances. As these industries continue to evolve, especially with the expansion of electric vehicles and consumer electronics, the demand for plastics is expected to increase as well.

Despite the many applications of plastic, one of the most significant challenges remains the disposal and management of plastic waste. The recycling rate for plastics remains low, particularly for single-use plastics, which make up a large portion of plastic waste. The global recycling rate for plastic was estimated at just 9% in 2021, according to a study by Science Advances. As plastic production increases, it is unlikely that current recycling infrastructure will be able to keep up with the growing volume of plastic waste unless significant investments are made to improve recycling rates and technologies.

Additionally, the lifecycle of plastic is highly problematic. Most plastics are designed for short-term use, especially in the case of packaging materials, and are not easily recyclable. This contributes to a high volume of plastic waste ending up in landfills or the environment, where it persists for centuries. Without major changes in production, consumption, and waste management practices, the accumulation of plastic waste will continue to escalate.

The Potential Impact of Continued Plastic Pollution if Current Practices Remain Unchanged

If current trends in plastic production and waste management continue, the impact of plastic pollution on the environment, human health, and economies will likely be devastating. The following are some of the potential consequences.

Environmental Impact: Ocean Pollution and Ecosystem Disruption

One of the most visible and troubling consequences of plastic waste is its impact on the marine environment. Plastics that end up in the oceans break down into microplastics, which are ingested by marine life, leading to harmful effects on ecosystems. If current plastic waste trends continue, the amount of plastic in the ocean is expected to grow substantially. The Great Pacific Garbage Patch, which is a massive accumulation of plastic waste in the Pacific Ocean, currently covers an area larger than twice the size of France. By 2050, plastic could outweigh all the fish in the oceans, according to a report by the Ellen MacArthur Foundation.

The toxicity of plastics is also a major concern. Many plastics contain harmful chemicals, such as phthalates, BPA, and flame retardants, which can leach into the water and accumulate in the bodies of marine animals. These chemicals can disrupt the hormonal systems of animals and humans alike, causing reproductive and developmental problems. As plastic pollution in the oceans increases, the risk to marine biodiversity and the overall health of marine ecosystems will intensify, leading to the potential collapse of essential food chains.

Human Health Risks

The pervasive spread of microplastics is not limited to marine life; they are also entering the human food chain. Microplastics have been found in seafood, drinking water, and even airborne particles, meaning that humans are being exposed to plastic pollutants at an alarming rate. Ingested microplastics can cause internal inflammation, immune system disruption, and reproductive issues. While the long-term health effects of microplastic exposure are still being studied, the potential risks to human health are concerning, particularly as the levels of microplastics in the environment continue to rise.

Additionally, plastics in consumer products such as personal care items, cosmetics, and cleaning products often contain chemicals that can leach into the environment. These chemicals have been linked to a variety of health problems, including endocrine disruption, cancer, and neurological damage. If current plastic production and disposal practices continue, the accumulation of these harmful substances in the environment will pose increasing risks to public health.

Economic Costs

The economic impact of continued plastic pollution is significant, both in terms of the costs of cleaning up plastic waste and the broader economic losses associated with environmental degradation. The costs of cleaning up plastic waste, especially in urban areas and coastal regions, can be substantial. According to a report by the UNEP, the cost of plastic pollution on the global economy is estimated to be over $13 billion annually, factoring in cleanup costs, damage to ecosystems, and lost productivity in sectors such as tourism, fishing, and agriculture.

The fishing industry is particularly vulnerable to the impacts of plastic pollution. Ghost fishing gear—discarded nets, lines, and traps—continues to trap marine animals, causing significant losses in the fishing industry. In addition, plastic pollution harms the aesthetic appeal of beaches and coastal regions, which can lead to a decline in tourism revenues. If plastic waste continues to increase at its current rate, these industries will face ongoing challenges, potentially leading to job losses and economic instability in affected regions.

Climate Change Implications

Plastic production is an energy-intensive process, and most plastics are made from fossil fuels. As demand for plastic continues to grow, so too will the carbon emissions associated with its production. According to a 2020 report from the Center for International Environmental Law (CIEL), the plastic sector could account for 20% of global oil consumption and 15% of the global carbon budget by 2050 if current production trends continue. This increase in plastic production will exacerbate the climate crisis by contributing significantly to greenhouse gas emissions.

Moreover, as plastic waste accumulates in landfills, it can release harmful greenhouse gases such as methane, further contributing to global warming. Plastic waste in the oceans also has implications for climate change, as the breakdown of plastics can release carbon and toxic chemicals into the marine environment, which can impact oceanic carbon sequestration processes.

Innovative Solutions on the Horizon

As the world faces an ever-growing plastic waste crisis, the need for innovative solutions has never been more pressing. Future technological, scientific, and policy developments hold great promise in transforming how we produce, manage, and dispose of plastic. From advanced recycling technologies to the integration of AI and blockchain, these emerging solutions have the potential to address the inefficiencies in the current plastic waste management system and create sustainable pathways for the future. This section explores some of the most exciting innovations on the horizon and how they could revolutionize the way plastic waste is handled.

Future Technological and Scientific Developments

Chemical Recycling and Advanced Recycling Methods

One of the key challenges in managing plastic waste is the limited efficiency of traditional mechanical recycling, particularly for mixed or contaminated plastics. Most plastics cannot be easily sorted, cleaned, or processed using traditional recycling methods, leading to high contamination rates and low recycling yields. Chemical recycling, however, is an emerging technology that could significantly improve the recycling process.

Chemical recycling works by breaking down plastics into their molecular components, allowing them to be reused as raw materials for new plastic products. Unlike mechanical recycling, which involves physically melting and reshaping plastic, chemical recycling can handle a broader range of plastic types, including contaminated or multi-layered materials. This technology can potentially enable closed-loop recycling systems, where the same plastic can be continually recycled without degrading its quality.

Pyrolysis and gasification are two forms of chemical recycling gaining traction. Pyrolysis involves heating plastic waste in the absence of oxygen to break it down into smaller molecules, which can then be converted into fuels, oils, or new plastic materials. Gasification, on the other hand, turns plastic waste into synthetic gas, which can be used to produce chemicals or electricity. While still in the early stages of commercial implementation, chemical recycling holds the promise of increasing the recycling rate of plastic waste and reducing the need for virgin plastic production.

Biodegradable Plastics and Bioplastics

The development of biodegradable plastics and bioplastics presents a potential solution to the long-term environmental impact of plastic waste. Unlike conventional plastics, which can take hundreds of years to break down, biodegradable plastics are designed to decompose more rapidly when exposed to environmental conditions. These plastics are made from renewable resources, such as corn starch, sugarcane, or algae, rather than petroleum-based materials, and they offer the possibility of reducing plastic waste in landfills and oceans.

However, the widespread use of biodegradable plastics presents challenges as well. While they decompose more quickly than traditional plastics, they still require specific environmental conditions, such as high humidity or industrial composting facilities, to break down effectively. Furthermore, biodegradable plastics may not always decompose in marine environments, where they can still contribute to plastic pollution. Innovations in biodegradable plastic formulations, such as PHA (polyhydroxyalkanoates) and PLA (polylactic acid), are underway to enhance their durability, compostability, and overall environmental performance.

Algae-based plastics are another exciting innovation. Algae can be used to produce biodegradable packaging that decomposes in natural environments, providing an alternative to single-use plastic packaging. Startups like AlgiKnit and Loliware are already working on algae-based materials for use in various applications, from packaging to textiles. These biodegradable alternatives could help reduce plastic pollution, particularly in coastal areas where plastic waste often ends up in the ocean.

Plastic-Eating Bacteria and Enzymes

The concept of plastic-eating bacteria and enzymes is one of the most promising scientific developments in the fight against plastic pollution. Researchers have discovered several strains of bacteria and fungi capable of degrading plastics, particularly PET (polyethylene terephthalate), one of the most widely used plastics in bottles and textiles. These organisms break down plastic molecules into smaller, non-toxic components, which can then be metabolized or converted into useful products.

Ideonella sakaiensis, a bacterium discovered in 2016, is capable of breaking down PET plastic by secreting an enzyme called PETase. This discovery has sparked interest in harnessing these natural processes to create more efficient recycling methods. Additionally, researchers are exploring ways to optimize these bacteria and enzymes for industrial-scale plastic degradation, potentially enabling large-scale plastic recycling without the need for chemical additives.

Scientists are also experimenting with enzyme-based solutions that can break down a wide range of plastic polymers, making plastic waste more easily recyclable. For example, Carbios, a French biotech company, is developing an enzymatic process for recycling PET plastics into their monomers, which can then be reused to create new PET products. Enzymatic plastic recycling could revolutionize the plastic waste management industry by enabling more effective and scalable recycling solutions.

The Role of Emerging Technologies: AI, Blockchain, and More

As the plastic waste crisis grows, emerging technologies such as AI, blockchain, and Internet of Things (IoT) are playing increasingly important roles in optimizing waste management and recycling processes. These technologies are helping businesses, governments, and organizations improve the efficiency of plastic recycling, track plastic waste flows, and create a more transparent and accountable system for managing plastic pollution.

Artificial Intelligence in Plastic Waste Sorting

One of the key barriers to effective plastic recycling is the difficulty of sorting different types of plastic materials. The traditional recycling process often relies on manual labor or basic mechanical systems, which can result in contamination and inefficiencies.

However, AI is now being used to improve the sorting process. AI-powered systems can analyze and identify different types of plastic with greater accuracy and speed than humans.

Companies like AMP Robotics have developed AI-powered robots that can identify, separate, and sort plastic waste at high speeds. These systems use computer vision and machine learning algorithms to distinguish between different plastic types, colors, and shapes, ensuring that only recyclable plastics are sent to processing facilities. AI can also optimize waste management systems by predicting waste generation patterns and streamlining the collection and sorting process. By increasing the efficiency of recycling operations, AI can help boost recycling rates and reduce the amount of plastic waste that ends up in landfills or the environment.

Blockchain for Transparency and Accountability

Another promising technology is blockchain, which is being explored as a way to enhance the transparency and traceability of plastic waste management. Blockchain is a decentralized digital ledger that records transactions in an immutable and transparent manner. By tracking the movement of plastic products through their lifecycle—from production and consumption to recycling and disposal—blockchain can help improve the efficiency and accountability of the plastic waste management system.

Blockchain can also play a role in EPR schemes, where manufacturers are required to take responsibility for the disposal of their products. By using blockchain, governments and businesses can track the flow of plastic waste, ensuring that producers comply with recycling and waste management regulations. This system could help ensure that plastic waste is recycled properly and that companies are held accountable for their environmental impact.

The IoT in Waste Management

The IoT is another technology that holds promise for improving plastic waste management. IoT involves connecting physical objects, such as waste bins, sensors, and recycling facilities, to the internet, allowing them to communicate and share data. By using IoT technology, waste management systems can be optimized in real time, ensuring that plastic waste is collected, sorted, and processed more efficiently.

Smart waste bins equipped with IoT sensors can monitor the amount of plastic waste and send alerts when they are full, helping waste management companies optimize collection schedules and routes. IoT technology can also be used to track the composition of waste, ensuring that recyclables, including plastics, are properly separated from non-recyclable waste. In the future, IoT-enabled systems could allow consumers to track the recycling status of their plastic products, providing greater incentives for responsible waste disposal and recycling.

A Call for Global Action

The plastic waste crisis represents one of the most pressing environmental challenges of the 21st century. The sheer volume of plastic produced, consumed, and discarded each year, combined with the slow rate of recycling and the environmental damage it causes, demands urgent attention. While technological and scientific advancements offer promising solutions, these efforts alone will not be sufficient to address the problem. What is needed now is international cooperation and collective action at a global scale, combined with the mobilization of a new generation of environmental leaders. This section explores the urgency of global cooperation in tackling plastic pollution and the importance of empowering youth and next-generation leaders in driving change.

The Urgency of International Cooperation and Collective Action

Plastic pollution is a global issue that transcends national borders, affecting ecosystems, wildlife, and communities across the world.

The plastic waste produced in one country can travel thousands of miles across oceans, contaminating marine environments, harming biodiversity, and ultimately impacting human populations. As a result, international cooperation is essential to curb plastic pollution and prevent further environmental degradation. A fragmented, national approach is insufficient to address the scale of the problem—global collaboration is necessary to implement long-term, sustainable solutions.

The Need for Coordinated Global Policy and Action

International frameworks like the Basel Convention, which was amended in 2019 to include plastic waste, have made important strides toward regulating the global movement of plastic waste. However, these efforts need to be strengthened and expanded to create binding international agreements that establish universal standards for plastic production, consumption, and disposal. Governments must work together to develop cohesive policies that enforce reductions in plastic production, ban or limit the use of harmful single-use plastics, and promote effective recycling programs. The United Nations' Clean Seas Campaign is another example of global cooperation aimed at addressing marine plastic pollution through education, policy advocacy, and partnerships. Programs like these need to be expanded and implemented with greater urgency.

For real change to occur, international agreements should include stronger mechanisms for monitoring and enforcement, ensuring that countries adhere to global standards. Environmental justice must be at the heart of these agreements, as developing nations, which often lack the resources to manage plastic waste, suffer disproportionately from plastic pollution. Wealthier nations, which are major producers of plastic, must take greater responsibility for the waste generated by their consumption patterns, particularly through EPR policies that ensure companies bear the cost of managing plastic waste.

Global Collaboration Between Governments, Corporations, and
Civil Society

Addressing plastic waste is not only a task for governments, but also
for the private sector and civil society. The plastic industry,
including major corporations that manufacture plastic products, has a
significant role to play in reducing plastic production and
encouraging the transition to more sustainable materials. By
collaborating with governments and environmental organizations,
corporations can help drive innovation in sustainable packaging,
invest in recycling technologies, and adopt circular economy
principles.

Moreover, civil society organizations, grassroots movements, and
NGOs are essential partners in the fight against plastic pollution.
These organizations often serve as catalysts for change, advocating
for stricter regulations, raising awareness about plastic waste, and
implementing on-the-ground initiatives such as clean-ups, recycling
drives, and education campaigns. Governments and businesses must
support these efforts by investing in local communities and
infrastructure and by adopting policies that enable community-
driven solutions to plastic waste.

As plastic pollution continues to escalate, the urgency of
international cooperation becomes increasingly clear. The impact of
plastic waste on ecosystems, wildlife, and human health is profound,
and without coordinated action, the problem will only worsen.
Governments, businesses, and civil society must come together to
form a unified global front that prioritizes sustainability and
environmental protection. It is not enough for individual countries or
corporations to act in isolation; it is only through collective action
that we can achieve a sustainable future free from the devastating
impacts of plastic waste.

Mobilizing the Next Generation of Environmental Leaders

While international cooperation and collective action are critical, the success of global efforts to tackle plastic pollution also depends on empowering and mobilizing the next generation of environmental leaders. Young people, especially those from communities most affected by plastic pollution, have the energy, creativity, and passion needed to drive forward the necessary cultural and systemic changes.

The Power of Youth Activism

Youth-led movements, such as Fridays for Future, have demonstrated the power of young people in demanding urgent action on climate change and environmental degradation. Inspired by Greta Thunberg, these movements have mobilized millions of young people around the world to call for stronger climate action, environmental justice, and policy change. Similarly, young environmental activists are beginning to take a stand on plastic waste, pushing for reductions in plastic production, bans on single-use plastics, and more effective recycling systems. These movements are crucial in bringing global attention to the plastic waste crisis and ensuring that it remains a priority on the international agenda.

Young people are also increasingly involved in entrepreneurship and innovative solutions to plastic pollution. Startups led by young environmentalists are developing new materials, creating alternatives to plastic packaging, and establishing sustainable supply chains. By harnessing their creativity and entrepreneurial spirit, the next generation is playing a vital role in shaping the future of sustainable practices and innovations in waste management.\

Education and Empowerment for Future Leaders

In order to effectively tackle the plastic waste crisis, it is essential to educate and empower the next generation with the knowledge, skills, and tools to drive meaningful change. Education should begin at a young age, helping children and young adults understand the environmental consequences of plastic pollution and the importance of reducing plastic consumption. Schools, universities, and community organizations should focus on teaching sustainability, environmental science, and circular economy principles, while also encouraging students to become active participants in local environmental initiatives. Through education, young people will be equipped to make informed decisions, challenge unsustainable practices, and advocate for policy changes at the local, national, and international levels.

Universities and research institutions also play a key role in preparing the next generation of environmental leaders. By conducting research on new materials, recycling technologies, and sustainable waste management systems, academic institutions are shaping the future of plastic waste solutions. Additionally, academic partnerships between universities and industry can foster innovation and help young leaders gain hands-on experience in developing and implementing solutions to plastic pollution.

Youth Engagement in Policy and Governance

It is also crucial to involve young people in policy-making and governance to ensure that the voices of future generations are heard in discussions about plastic waste and sustainability. Governments and international organizations should create platforms and opportunities for young people to engage in decision-making processes related to environmental policies. This could include youth councils, advisory committees, or internships within governmental and intergovernmental agencies. By involving young leaders in the development of policies and strategies, we ensure that solutions are not only effective but also equitable, considering the long-term implications for future generations.

Moreover, as the next generation becomes more engaged in environmental governance, they will bring fresh perspectives and innovative ideas to solving complex environmental challenges, including plastic pollution. Their involvement will be essential in driving the policy changes needed to create a sustainable future, from promoting circular economy practices to instituting global plastic waste reduction targets.

The fight against plastic pollution is a global challenge that requires urgent and sustained action. International cooperation, collective policy efforts, and the mobilization of the next generation of environmental leaders are essential for creating a sustainable future. The need for global agreements, innovative technologies, and youth-driven activism has never been more urgent. By fostering collaboration across sectors and empowering young people to become environmental leaders, we can work together to mitigate the plastic waste crisis and create a world where sustainability and environmental stewardship are prioritized.

The next generation holds the power to shape the future of our planet, and as the world rallies together to combat plastic pollution, their voices, actions, and creativity will be critical in driving the changes needed to build a cleaner, healthier, and more sustainable world for all.

Conclusion

In this final chapter, we summarize the key insights and solutions presented throughout the book, reflecting on the urgency of addressing the plastic waste crisis. The conclusion highlights the importance of collaborative global action, innovative technologies, and sustainable practices in reducing plastic pollution. It calls for a collective effort across governments, industries, and communities to implement effective policies and responsible production methods. Additionally, the chapter emphasizes the role of individuals and the next generation of environmental leaders in driving lasting change. As we close, we reaffirm that a comprehensive, unified approach is essential to creating a future where plastic waste is minimized, and sustainability is at the forefront of decision-making across all sectors.

Summarizing the Key Takeaways from the Book

The plastic waste crisis is one of the most urgent environmental challenges of our time. Over the past century, the production and consumption of plastic have escalated to unprecedented levels, with global plastic production expected to more than double by 2050. This increase in plastic use has resulted in a staggering rise in plastic waste, much of which is not recycled or disposed of properly. The environmental, human health, and economic impacts of plastic waste are profound, affecting ecosystems, wildlife, and human communities across the globe.

Throughout this book, we have explored the multifaceted nature of the plastic waste crisis and presented a wide range of solutions and innovative approaches to address it. Here are the key takeaways that emerge from the chapters:

1. The Scale of the Plastic Waste Crisis

The book has highlighted the immense scale of the global plastic waste problem. Over 300 million metric tons of plastic are produced annually, and a significant portion of this ends up in landfills or the environment. Much of the plastic waste is single-use or short-lived, leading to long-term pollution, particularly in marine environments. The book demonstrates that the crisis is not only an environmental issue but also a threat to human health, as plastic waste contaminates food, water, and air with harmful chemicals.

2. Innovative Solutions Are Key to Reducing Plastic Waste

The book underscores the importance of technological innovation in tackling the plastic waste crisis. Advanced recycling methods, such as chemical recycling, offer promising solutions for managing plastic waste that cannot be processed using traditional methods. Additionally, biodegradable plastics and alternative materials made from renewable sources like algae and bamboo can help reduce reliance on petroleum-based plastics. Further research and development in these areas are essential for creating sustainable alternatives and improving recycling efficiency.

3. The Importance of Global Cooperation and Policy Reform

As plastic waste is a global issue, it requires international cooperation to address effectively. The book emphasizes the need for stronger global agreements to regulate plastic production and waste, such as the Basel Convention and the United Nations Clean Seas Campaign. At the national level, policies such as plastic bag bans, EPR laws, and deposit return schemes are already proving effective in reducing plastic waste. The book argues that the success of these policies relies on robust enforcement and international collaboration.

4. The Role of Businesses and Industries

Corporations and industries play a central role in addressing plastic pollution. Through corporate responsibility, sustainable packaging innovations, and investment in circular economy models, businesses can significantly reduce their environmental footprint. The book showcases examples of businesses that are leading the way in plastic reduction, such as Unilever and Coca-Cola, which are moving toward recyclable, biodegradable, or plant-based packaging. Public-private partnerships are essential for driving widespread change and scaling solutions.

5. Grassroots Movements and Community Action

The book also highlights the power of community-led initiatives in combating plastic waste. Grassroots movements, such as Plastic Free July, have gained global traction, empowering individuals and communities to reduce their plastic consumption. Local clean-up programs and waste-to-energy technologies in developing countries are showing that small-scale, community-driven efforts can have a significant impact. These movements not only address local waste but also create awareness and build momentum for larger systemic changes.

6. Mobilizing the Next Generation of Environmental Leaders

The future of the plastic waste movement rests in the hands of the next generation. Young activists and entrepreneurs are already leading the charge for change, pushing for policy reforms, corporate accountability, and more sustainable practices. The book stresses the importance of education and empowerment to equip young leaders with the tools and knowledge to tackle the plastic crisis. It calls for greater involvement of youth in decision-making processes, as their voices will be instrumental in shaping future policies and innovations.

7. A Call for Urgent Action

The book concludes with a call for urgent, collective action to reduce plastic waste. The crisis demands an immediate shift in how plastics are produced, used, and disposed of. Governments, businesses, and individuals must collaborate to create a sustainable, circular economy that minimizes plastic waste and maximizes the reuse and recycling of materials. The future of our planet depends on the decisions we make today.

In summary, while the plastic waste crisis is daunting, it is not insurmountable. Through innovation, policy reform, corporate responsibility, and grassroots movements, we can take meaningful steps toward a sustainable future. The solutions outlined in this book are just the beginning, and with collective effort, the global community can significantly reduce plastic waste and protect the environment for future generations. The time to act is now.

The Need for Collaboration, Innovation, and Systemic Change to Address the Plastic Waste Crisis

The plastic waste crisis represents one of the most pressing environmental challenges of the 21st century. With over 300 million tons of plastic produced annually, the overwhelming majority of which is not recycled, plastic waste has become ubiquitous in both terrestrial and marine environments. The consequences are dire: wildlife harm, ecosystem disruption, pollution of our oceans, and a growing burden on public health. To tackle this crisis, it is clear that collaboration, innovation, and systemic change are essential.

Collaboration Across Sectors and Borders

Plastic waste knows no boundaries. It travels across national borders, impacting countries and ecosystems far from where it was originally produced. Therefore, addressing the plastic crisis requires global cooperation. Governments must work together to establish international frameworks, such as the Basel Convention, which already governs the transboundary movement of hazardous waste, including plastics. Countries need to align on common policies, such as bans on single-use plastics, EPR, and mandatory recycling targets. A collaborative effort, facilitated by international organizations like the UNEP, is critical to ensure universal standards for plastic waste management.

At the same time, private industry and public sector partnerships are equally important. Businesses have the resources to innovate in packaging and material design, yet they often lack the regulatory framework or incentives to make significant changes. PPPs can provide the necessary leverage to create scalable solutions that address both the production of plastic and its end-of-life management. Governments can incentivize sustainable business practices, and corporations, in turn, can drive technological innovation. For example, the use of biodegradable plastics, advanced recycling technologies, and reusable packaging systems can be promoted through these collaborations.

Innovation in Technology and Materials

Innovation will play a central role in mitigating the impact of plastic waste. Traditional recycling methods are ineffective for many plastic products, particularly those made from mixed or contaminated materials. Chemical recycling and biological plastic degradation technologies offer promising alternatives by allowing the recycling of a broader range of plastics and reducing the need for virgin plastic production.

Moreover, biodegradable plastics and alternative materials, such as plant-based plastics and algae-based packaging, provide sustainable substitutes to petroleum-derived plastics. Research and development in these areas are crucial to scaling these solutions, ensuring they are not only effective but also cost-competitive with conventional plastics. Governments, industries, and academia must work together to accelerate the commercial viability of these alternatives.

Systemic Change in Consumption and Disposal

Finally, to truly solve the plastic waste crisis, there must be systemic change in how plastics are produced, consumed, and disposed of.

The current linear economy model—where plastic is used once and discarded—needs to shift towards a circular economy. In this model, plastics are recycled, reused, or repurposed to create new products, reducing waste and conserving resources. For such a transition, governments must create policies that encourage responsible consumption, reduce plastic waste, and prioritize recycling and waste minimization.

Public education and behavioral change are key components of this systemic shift. Citizens must be made aware of the environmental impacts of plastic waste and empowered to make more sustainable choices, such as reducing plastic usage, choosing reusable alternatives, and properly disposing of plastic waste. Such efforts, alongside improved infrastructure for waste collection and recycling, will help create a more responsible, circular plastic economy.

Final Thoughts on the Role of Individuals, Industries, and Governments in Creating a Sustainable Future Without Plastic Waste

As we confront the ever-growing plastic waste crisis, the path to a sustainable future lies in the combined efforts of individuals, industries, and governments. Each of these groups has a unique role to play, and their collaboration is critical in achieving a future where plastic waste is minimized, recycling is maximized, and sustainable alternatives are the norm. In this final reflection, we consider the specific responsibilities and actions that each group must take to tackle plastic waste and create lasting environmental change.

The Role of Individuals

At the core of any meaningful environmental change is individual action. Consumers have tremendous power in shaping demand for products and services, and their choices can influence industries to adopt more sustainable practices. Individual responsibility begins with reducing plastic consumption and choosing alternatives that have less environmental impact. Reusable bags, water bottles, and packaging-free products can become the standard for many consumers, especially if they prioritize sustainability in their purchasing decisions. These seemingly small actions, when practiced on a large scale, can significantly reduce the demand for single-use plastics.

Moreover, individuals can advocate for change in their communities and beyond. Engaging in local clean-up efforts, participating in recycling programs, and supporting policy initiatives that push for stronger environmental regulations are all essential components of active citizenship. As environmental awareness continues to grow, individuals have the opportunity to raise awareness, educate others, and promote sustainable lifestyles through their personal networks and social media. The power of grassroots movements, from local campaigns to global movements like Fridays for Future, shows how collective action can spark significant change. In this sense, individuals have the power to influence both culture and policy, encouraging broader societal shifts toward sustainability.

The Role of Industries

Industries play a pivotal role in the fight against plastic waste, as they are the primary producers and consumers of plastic products. Corporate responsibility is essential in reducing plastic pollution. By adopting circular economy models, companies can minimize waste and keep materials in use for as long as possible. This includes designing products for reuse, repair, and recycling, as well as adopting sustainable materials and reducing reliance on single-use plastics. Many companies are already making strides in this direction by investing in biodegradable packaging, recycled plastics, and alternative materials, showing that sustainable innovation can coexist with profitability.

Furthermore, industries must take responsibility for the entire lifecycle of their products through EPR schemes. These policies hold manufacturers accountable for the recycling and disposal of their products, incentivizing them to design for sustainability and recyclability. Public-private partnerships are critical in this process, as industry leaders can collaborate with governments and NGOs to create efficient recycling systems and waste management infrastructures. Through these efforts, industries can significantly reduce plastic waste and shift toward more sustainable production practices.

The Role of Governments

Governments are the backbone of effective plastic waste management. They have the authority to implement regulations and policies that create the structural changes needed to reduce plastic waste at a large scale. These include plastic bans, recycling mandates, and EPR programs that hold corporations accountable for plastic waste. Governments can also provide incentives for businesses that adopt sustainable practices, such as tax breaks for companies that reduce plastic use or invest in new recycling technologies.

Governments must also invest in infrastructure, ensuring that waste management systems are in place to properly recycle and dispose of plastic products. Public education campaigns are essential in raising awareness about plastic waste and encouraging responsible consumption. International cooperation is equally important; plastic pollution is a global issue, and countries must collaborate through treaties and agreements to reduce plastic waste worldwide.

Collaboration and Systems Change

While individual, industrial, and governmental efforts are crucial, true progress can only be made through collaboration. The fight against plastic waste is not a solitary endeavor but a global challenge that requires the collective effort of all sectors. Governments must create the policies that guide industries and individuals toward sustainable practices, while businesses must innovate and adopt those policies in their production processes. Individuals, in turn, can drive demand for sustainable products, pushing businesses to continue evolving and holding governments accountable for enforcing regulations.

A systems change is needed—one that shifts away from the traditional linear economy, where plastics are produced, consumed, and discarded, and towards a circular economy that prioritizes reducing, reusing, and recycling. This systemic transformation will require the cooperation of all stakeholders, from individuals to governments, to create a world where plastic waste is no longer a burden on the planet but a resource to be reused and recycled.

Conclusion

In conclusion, creating a sustainable future without plastic waste is an ambitious but achievable goal. It requires the collective effort of individuals, industries, and governments to adopt sustainable practices, invest in innovative technologies, and implement effective policies. While individual actions can reduce consumption and raise awareness, industries must shift their production methods to prioritize sustainability, and governments must create the regulatory frameworks and infrastructure to support these changes. The road ahead will not be easy, but through collaboration, innovation, and systemic change, we can build a world where plastic waste no longer poses a threat to our environment and future generations. The time to act is now, and each of us has a role to play.

www.ingramcontent.com/pod-product-compliance
Lightning Source LLC
Chambersburg PA
CBHW052136270326
41930CB00012B/2913